US

AGAINST
THE WORLD

Before Saying, "I DO"...
Knowing True Love

US
AGAINST
THE WORLD

Before Saying, "I DO"...
Knowing True Love

CATHERINE HARMON

HUNTER ENTERTAINMENT NETWORK

Colorado Springs, Colorado

To order products, or for any other correspondence:

Hunter Entertainment Network
4164 Austin Bluffs Parkway, Suite 214
Colorado Springs, Colorado 80918
www.hunter-ent-net.com
Tel. (253) 906-2160 – Fax: (719) 528-6359
E-mail: contact@hunter-entertainment.com
Or reach us on Facebook at: Hunter Entertainment Network
"Offering God's Heart to a Dying World"

This book and all other Hunter Entertainment Network™ Hunter Heart Publishing™, and Hunter Heart Kids™ books are available at Christian bookstores and distributors worldwide.

Chief Editor: Gord Dormer
Book cover design: Phil Coles Independent Design
Layout & logos: Exousia Marketing Group www.exousiamg.com
ISBN: 978-1-937741-15-0
Printed in the United States of America.

DEDICATION

This book is dedicated to the many that have fallen into a marriage relationship that was not directed under God's guidance, including my very own marriage. After the many talks with those couples whose marriage did not make it into oneness and the marriages that claim to be in misery, still today, it gives me a deep passion to give the wisdom needed to those thinking about marrying, so that before saying, "I do," will examine their relationship with God and their mate. God does not intend for marriages to ever end in divorce, but He also does not intend for you to not marry His best for you. In the beginning, God made man and woman so they can become one flesh. That means He has a best for you and if we marry His best, then He intends us to stay married for life. Let's stop the cycle of not receiving God's best when choosing a lifetime mate, so that we can overcome the divorce rate.

Acknowledgements

I would like to give acknowledgement to the following people who have supported the writing that is a part of my healing for the journey I am currently experiencing. My journey is mine in truth and I am so excited to be able to share it through my writing, in hopes that it is answered prayer for someone else.

Deborah Hunter and staff

All those who purchased the first book of this series and those who tuned into the radio shows bright and early in the mornings, I hope you received some insight from it.

Delicia and Christopher Mckinney-Gospel Radio Nation

Latricia Willis-Laprimera1220am

My family: Fe and James Newkirk, Jermaine and Tasha Phillips, Joseph Phillips, and Jaden and Jayla Harmon. Thank you for encouraging me every step of the way.

My friends: For sharing your deepest concerns, heartaches, and joys in your relationships and encouragement through mine, during and after.

My counselors: Giving me insight for each step I take and helping me see God in all this.

Table of Contents

Chapter 1

What is Love?

"Love is patient, love is kind. It does not envy, it does not boast, it is not proud. It does not dishonor others, it is not self-seeking, it is not easily angered, it keeps no record of wrongs. Love does not delight in evil but rejoices with the truth. It always protects, always trusts, always hopes, always perseveres."

(1 Corinthians 13:4-7, NIV)

*I*f you have not already familiarized yourself with this scripture, then please read it, observe it, and keep it in your heart. There is no better definition of love than this. This love is not temporary, a game-piece, or something that you learn over night. It is love that is displayed in a home; it is love that can be modeled off of; it is love that can be learned and taught. But, the most important thing to know about this love is that it should be genuine and easily demonstrated in yourself and your future spouse. This kind of love is pure in heart and shows character in an individual. So, when you feel you are in love with a person that you want to marry, understand the definition of *real love* from God's Word.

Too many of us fall in love with someone, not knowing what is the true meaning of love. We may not know what love is because it may not have been modeled in our own home or ever experienced. Whatever the reason is, God clearly tells us His definition of what love is and there is no one better to give that definition, because He Himself is *Love*. Some of the characteristics of this kind of love have been demonstrated by several people throughout the Bible, but all of these characteristics of love have been demonstrated by God Himself, both as Father and Man, whom we know as Jesus. These characteristics of love defined who Jesus was and He was perfect in being, teaching, and showing this kind of love. Let's take a look at how He demonstrated these characteristics of love and define them in detail.

Love is Patient

"She will give birth to a son, and you are to give him the name Jesus, because he will save his people from their sins."

(Matthew 1:21, NIV)

"The Lord is not slow to fulfill his promise as some count slowness, but is patient toward you, not wishing that any should perish, but that all should reach repentance."

(2 Peter 3:9, NIV)

Before Jesus was even born, it was pre-destined that He would be the Messiah who saves all of us from the world. He was born specifically for that mission and it was to be fulfilled. However, did it happen as soon as He was born? No, but His ultimate mission to die on the cross for us did not take place until He was thirty-three years old. Can you imagine that? For His time here on earth, He knew exactly what His mission was, but He could not make time pass fast enough to accomplish that. Did He wait in agony for that moment? Not at all. In fact, He spent time with God and had a strong desire to be in His Heavenly Father's house as often as He could, gaining wisdom and favor with God (Luke 2:49-52). Now, what makes this even more fascinating is the fact that Jesus knew His purpose was to die for all of us. Who would anticipate and look forward to that mission? That mission does not seem appealing to any of us. But, Jesus patiently waited for that moment, because He knew that His purpose was not about Him, but about us.

Even today, long after His mission has been completed, He is patient with all of us, even when we are not at our best. While we continue to be ourselves in our own flesh, or while we choose not to trust Him, He just patiently awaits us, until we are ready. He does not pressure us to hurry up or manipulate us to choose His ways; He patiently waits while He gives us subtle whispers to come to Him. You could be six-years-old or fifty-years-old; you could be a teenager trying to figure out life or a seventy-year-old who lived a long life; you could be at a very high point in your life or at the darkest place of your life; no matter who or where you are, Jesus is always waiting for you to simply be with Him and choose Him. He is so very patient with us, and there is nothing we can or cannot do that will keep Him from waiting on us. Do you know why He patiently waits? It's because He has the best for us and He wants to give it to us. We are worth so much to Him and He thinks we are worth waiting for. Jesus is not waiting for you to stop doing what you are doing; He is waiting for you to basically say, "I do". I do accept You into my life; I do trust You in all things; I do want a relationship with You; I do believe in You; I do receive Your grace and mercy; *I do, I do, I do*. He is waiting for the best thing to happen when you say, "I do".

We all want to see great things happen and that is what patience does, it waits and anticipates for the best things to happen. However, during the waiting period is where true character is shown. As I stated earlier, Jesus knew what His mission was all His life, and during His long time of waiting, He was not complaining, worrying, getting frustrated, or trying to speed up the process. He does not do that with us now, either. In order to observe a person's patience, observe the waiting period that they are in. It could be anything as little as them waiting on you to make up your mind on something or anything more challenging like waiting on a job promotion. The waiting period is where things about a person, or even yourself, are revealed and how you handle situations. The waiting period speaks volumes and is a learning season. When Jesus went to His Father's house, it was the moment where He gained wisdom while He was waiting for His mission to take place.

"The end of a matter is better than its beginning, and patience is better than pride."

(Ecclesiastes 7:8, NIV)

Patience is definitely needed with one another as a couple. I am not just talking about dealing with a *bridezilla* during the wedding planning or dealing with a groom-to-be's choice of bachelor party. Each of you are going to have flaws, or come across circumstances and decisions that will need to take place that will require patience from one another or to each other. Having a glimpse of what type of patience one has and how they handle circumstances during the waiting period, will allow you to gain insight of what you will be dealing with during the first years of your marriage and probably for years after. Your years together will also require you to have patience towards your mate. Patience will grow and get easier the more time you spend together, but if the patience you are observing as an engaged couple isn't starting off positive, then really think about how it can hinder your growth. When dealing with one another, patience is definitely better than pride.

When a person is proud, they are likely not able to accept anything other than their own expectations, without the consideration of others. They are often focused on how the world has to revolve around them and believe that they are entitled to or deserving of it. It is very hard to deal with prideful people, because they often do not want to learn anything about themselves or others to produce growth, and can lack the humility that is needed to empathize with other people. Patience is always better than pride.

Patience is willing to bear all things until the very end, because of the end result. Patience is always willing to wait, learn, deal in a productive manner, and expect an outcome that will be pleasing to self and others. God displayed a great deal of patience and aren't you so glad that He is a very patient God!

Reflection Questions:

Question 1: How do you feel that you are patient? Does your mate agree with you? Why or why not?

Question 2: Name two ways that you have witnessed your mate being patient. Why did those stand out to you?

Question 3: Name two ways that you have witnessed your mate being impatient. How do you think that impatience can affect your relationship in the long run?

Love is Kind

"So he came to a town in Samaria called Sychar, near the plot of ground Jacob had given to his son Joseph. Jacob's well was there, and Jesus, tired as he was from the journey, sat down by the well. It was about noon. When a Samaritan woman came to draw water, Jesus said to her, "Will you give me a drink?" (His disciples had gone into the town to buy food.) The Samaritan woman said to him, "You are a Jew and I am a Samaritan woman. How can you ask me for a drink?" (For Jews do not associate with Samaritans.) Jesus answered her, "If you knew the gift of God and who it is that asks you for a drink, you would have asked him and he would have given you living water." "Sir," the woman said, "you have nothing to draw with and the well is deep. Where can you get this living water? Are you greater than our father Jacob, who gave us the well and drank from it himself, as did also his sons and his livestock? Jesus answered, "Everyone who drinks this water will be thirsty again, but whoever drinks the water I give them will never thirst. Indeed, the water I give them will become in them a spring of water welling up to eternal life."The woman said to him, "Sir, give me this water so that I won't get thirsty and have to keep coming here to draw water."He told her, "Go, call your husband and come back." "I have no husband," she replied. Jesus said to her, "You are right when you say you have no husband. The fact is, you have had five husbands, and the man you now have is not your husband. What you have just said is quite true."

(John 4: 5-18, NIV)

I wanted to point out this story to show you how Jesus demonstrated His kindness in two ways. The first way is to show that He is kind to all people, no matter what racial or ethnic background they are from. During that time period, Jews and Samaritans were not to associate themselves with each other. There was a strong hatred between them and if anyone was caught talking to the other, condemnation was brought on them. But, Jesus had no hang-ups about who He wanted to reach. He could have ignored the woman at the well and kept His distance from her. Instead, He kindly spoke to her and asked for a drink. Now keep in mind, that if Jesus could walk on water, then surely He could have retrieved His own drink if He really desired. So, His intention to speak to the Samaritan woman was not to get a drink. He had another motive in speaking to her. Jesus already knew everything about this woman before she even spoke to Him. In fact, it was not a coincidence that she was there to get offered *living water*. After Jesus told her about this *living water*, she was desperate to have it, so that she would never thirst again. Little did she know that Jesus was going to offer her *water* that would not allow her to ever thirst again for another husband more than Him. He knew about her five husbands and the one she was with that was not her husband. It is not clear to us why this woman had five husbands, but I can guarantee you that while reading her story, you may have formulated in your mind the reason. Some of us may have even condemned her for having five husbands. If you did, that is just part of how we view things in the flesh. Truth is that back in those days, it was not lawful for a wife to divorce a husband; it was only lawful for a husband to divorce a wife. Apparently, there was something about this woman that men did not value in her that led them to divorce. We do not know what it is or why, but, look closely at how Jesus responded to her request for the *living water*. He tells her that she can have it, but to go get her husband and bring him back. Could Jesus have given her the *living water* without her husband? Of course, but He was setting her up to come to know Him. Not only was He setting her up to come to know who He was, but He was doing it in a kind way. He could have condemned her. He could have questioned why she had five husbands and why she was with one who was not her husband. He could have pointed out the shame for having six different men, but He didn't. He was kind enough not to make her feel bad about who she was; instead, He offered her something that would supersede all her relationships, which was Him.

Being kind means being benevolent by nature in consideration of others; mild, gentle, and helpful. You have heard the expression, "a little kindness goes a long way." Look at the little kindness that Jesus showed the Samaritan woman. It was a seed that would then spread to others in the Samaritan culture, which would eventually bring them to the mercy of the Messiah. "A little kindness goes a long way."

Being kind to one another does so much more than we think it does. Being kind can diminish an angry person's heart, it can brighten up a person's day, it can open up a person to conversation, it can make a person feel cherished or loved, it can build another up, it can encourage, and it can produce kindness in others. Being kind is also good and makes your spirit bear fruit and brings joy to our Father. Kindness is contagious and without it, a person can be rude, cruel, unmindful, thoughtless, or unsympathetic. So, when you offer the opposite of kindness, you can put everyone around you in a dampened mood. Who wants to be around someone who is not kind, only to jeopardize their own spirit?

Kindness is definitely a characteristic that is needed in a relationship. There will be times when the flaws in each other will be magnified, or times when one is having an unpleasant day and taking it out on whomever, or times when you simply will not agree on issues. It's during those times when we can get frustrated and want to poke someone's eyeballs out. It's perfectly normal to feel angry or frustrated, but how you respond to each other makes a world of difference. The saying, "kill them with kindness," has a pretty simple meaning. In our own natural flesh, we want to retaliate and point out all that is wrong by lashing out and back. However, doing so will only escalate more harsh feelings. But, when we speak to each other with kindness, so much more can be recognized, resolved, and accomplished.

Reflection Questions

Question 1: How often does your mate show kindness toward you? How does it make you feel?

Question 2: Name an action that you did towards your mate that was unkind? What did your action lead to? What would have been a better outcome if you used kindness?

It Does Not Envy

"And God spoke all these words: "I am the LORD your God, who brought you out of Egypt, out of the land of slavery. "You shall have no other gods before me. "You shall not make for yourself an image in the form of anything in heaven above or on the earth beneath or in the waters below. You shall not bow down to them or worship them; for I, the LORD your God, am a jealous God, punishing the children for the sin of the parents to the third and fourth generation of those who hate me. "

(Exodus 20:1-5, NIV)

Many of us have heard the term, *God is a jealous God.* It's written in Exodus 20:5. It is often misunderstood how we believe God to be envious. We know envy to be feelings of dissatisfaction or covetousness with regard to another person's advantages, achievements, or belongings. Envy is being dissatisfied with what you have and wanting what others have. This definition of envy does not quite fit the characteristic of God, because number one, He is love; but more importantly, number two, He is owner of everything. So, there is literally nothing that He has to be envious about since the entire Universe is His anyway. So, God does not envy. Well, what does it mean that He is a jealous God then? In Exodus 20:5, God delivered the Israelites from their bondage to slavery. Only God did the seemingly impossible and because of that, He deserves the glory. But, when the Israelites were looking for a god to glorify their release from bondage, they started worshipping a cow made out of gold and jewelry. This made God very angry because why on earth would they worship a cow who had absolutely nothing to do with their freedom from slavery? He is telling them not to give the glory to anyone else, but Him. If He is Creator of all; Omnipotent, Omnipresent, and Omniscient, then He wants the glory for it all. He is loyal to all His children to make sure that He provides, protects, and loves. But, when we glorify ourselves or glorify other idols, then it robs God of everything He is to us. Let's make it clear one more time, God does not envy; He simply wants the glory where glory is due.

When I was in a dark place in my life, I kept hearing the words, "God wants all the glory." I began to question that and ask why He wants the glory so much. In my first book, I explained why God wants the glory in everything. The answer that was revealed to me was that He wants the glory, because His glory is our blessing. He is not envious because He wants something that He does not have; He is envious, or jealous, that He did not get the glory for the blessing He gave you.

Take for example, when a man is ready to propose to the woman he loves; he may want to make it a very spectacular event. He gets all the details in place to make sure that it will be an amazing surprise. He created this well thought out event to make it the most special moment for the woman he loves. The place is perfect, the timing is perfect, the ring is perfect, the words in his heart are perfect, and his plan is made perfect. When it happens, he hopes for the best. Okay, it's time and everything worked out so far, just as he planned. Now, comes the big moment and it is time to propose, "Will you marry me?" The expected outcome is "Yes, I will marry you!" However, what if she said something else instead? Something like, "Well, you did pretty good, but I liked how Nick proposed to Vanessa on the Bachelor. His was the best proposal ever." How on earth do you think this young man would feel? Probably feels like cursing Nick out for being the television idol that his girlfriend admired more than him. Perhaps, he would have a big gunk of chunk in his throat that his girlfriend actually said that; probably, anger, disbelief, and many other negative feelings. The fact that this young man went through all he did to make that special moment for his girlfriend a special blessed event, and was ruined because of a television idol. Where's the credit for what he attempted to do? This is how God feels when you give the glory to others, instead of to Him. He wants to bless you in every way with all that He has for you, so when He says He is a jealous God, then He is rightfully so when you glorify others for what you have that was given to you by Him.

"At one time we too were foolish, disobedient, deceived and enslaved by all kinds of passions and pleasures. We lived in malice and envy, being hated and hating one another."

(Titus 3:3, NIV)

What can we say about love that does not envy? When a couple is in love with one another, then they are not in competition with each other. They give each other credit where credit is due, and they find confidence in one another to help build each other up. Envious people have deep rooted issues within themselves that make them feel like they have to compete against something they wish they had and don't have. We all have passions and pleasures within us that we would like to see fulfilled, and there is nothing wrong with having that. However, we all have to work at receiving them, but while we are waiting to receive them, do not envy someone else because they already have them. As couples, we should not be envious of the other's accomplishments; instead, we should celebrate with them and find out what we can do to help them reach their very best. The relationship can be strained when envy takes place. You have seen it when husbands are envious, because their wives are making more money than they are; when wives are envious, because the kids seem to have more fun with their dad; when a spouse is more humorous than the other; when one cooks better than the other; etc. If we focus on what is better to have than what we have for or in ourselves, then envy will destroy us. So, take the time to value what the other has out of love and give them the credit that they deserve for being who they are.

Reflection Questions:

Question 1: What can your mate do that is better than you? Do you appreciate that or envy it? Why do you appreciate it or envy it?

Question 2: Is there any area in your relationship where you feel like you are competing with your mate? How can you help each other lessen that competition?

Question 3: What would you like your mate to do to help you accomplish your full potential?

It Does Not Boast

"Then they all took Jesus to Pilate and began to bring up charges against him. They said, "We found this man undermining our law and order, forbidding taxes to be paid to Caesar, setting himself up as Messiah-King." Pilate asked him, "Is this true that you're 'King of the Jews'?" "Those are your words, not mine," Jesus replied. Pilate told the high priests and the accompanying crowd, "I find nothing wrong here. He seems harmless enough to me." But they were vehement. "He's stirring up unrest among the people with his teaching, disturbing the peace everywhere, starting in Galilee and now all through Judea. He's a dangerous man, endangering the peace." When Pilate heard that, he asked, "So, he's a Galilean?" Realizing that he properly came under Herod's jurisdiction, he passed the buck to Herod, who just happened to be in Jerusalem for a few days. Herod was delighted when Jesus showed up. He had wanted for a long time to see him, he'd heard so much about him. He hoped to see him do something spectacular. He peppered him with questions. Jesus didn't answer—not one word. But the high priests and religion scholars were right there, saying their piece, strident and shrill in their accusations.

(Luke 23: 1-10, MSG)

When Jesus was brought to Pilate and Herod, He was being questioned as to who He was. When asked if He was the King of the Jews, Jesus could have said He is the Messiah, but instead, He responds in a way to let them know that it is, indeed, who they say He is. Herod was anticipating that Jesus would perform miraculous things to prove who He was and is claimed to be. Jesus could have very well done something spectacular and boastful to prove who He was, but Jesus already knew that it was not going to matter what He said or did, because it was going to be taken as disbelief by the men anyway. There was no need to boast, because Jesus is who He says He is and since He was confident in His purpose and mission, He humbled

11

Himself to what needed to be done to fulfill what was written. He focused on His mission to show His love for us.

"This is what the LORD says: "Let not the wise boast of their wisdom or the strong boast of their strength or the rich boast of their riches, but let the one who boasts boast about this: that they have the understanding to know me, that I am the LORD, who exercises kindness, justice and righteousness on earth, for in these I delight," declares the LORD."

(Jeremiah 9:23-24, NIV)

There is a fine line between sharing excitement about your blessings and boasting. God surely knows how to bless us in ways that can make us shout "Hallelujah!" There is nothing wrong with being excited for what you have or who God created you to be. God blessed you with your characteristics, ability, gifts, talents, monetary items, and status. So, we should be able to be excited about those blessings and share. However, we should not share it in a boastful way. Now that we have social media, it makes it very easy to boast about what we have been given. Social media is the generation where we can create our own image and glamorize our existence. But, God tells us not to boast about these things in such a way that glorifies or exalts ourselves; if we are going to boast, then make sure you are boasting about how good God is and how He is the one who is in control of your everything. Not only does God bless you with the things just mentioned, but He also blesses you with personal accomplishments, deliverance, healing, strength, opportunities, and other things that only you and God know about. It is these things that helped you come to a realization of how good God is to you personally, so you can bless others by boasting about how good God is.

When you are being boastful about yourself and everything you have to glorify yourself, the only motive behind that is to make others feel bad and make you feel good. Boasting to make you feel and look good discredits the goodness of God. We are living in a dying world and people are searching for answers to the dark areas in their lives, so the one person that we, as Christians, should be directing them to is Jesus. When we boast to give ourselves the glory, then we rob people of the opportunity to be directed to the one who can give them their answers in truth. Stay focused on the purpose of why you received what you have from Him. Just like Jesus, He stayed focus on His mission and that was for us to have this amazing relationship with Him.

In a relationship with our mate, we should not boast to one another either. We should not make ourselves look better than the other person. We are going to have different characteristics, gifts, talents, etc., that set ourselves apart from each other, but we should not boast about it and make each other feel bad, so we can look or feel better than the other. It could be as little as a spouse boasting about how much better their cooking is compared to the other spouse; or something as big as a spouse boasting about how everything in the house, including the house was all provided, because of their own hard work and the other spouse did nothing to contribute. It could be a spouse boasting about how they were a better parent or that they do more for the community than the other.

Reflection Questions:

Question 1: What does your mate focus on to make themselves look good? Would you say that it is boastful and if so, do you think it is intentional?

Question 2: What area of your life do you feel like you can share with other people that may be a blessing to them? Do you feel like it was God-given or self-given?

Love is Not Proud

"*The evening meal was in progress, and the devil had already prompted Judas, the son of Simon Iscariot, to betray Jesus. Jesus knew that the Father had put all things under his power, and that he had come from God and was returning to God; so he got up from the meal, took off his outer clothing, and wrapped a towel around his waist. After that, he poured water into a basin and began to wash his disciples' feet, drying them with the towel that was wrapped around him.*

He came to Simon Peter, who said to him, "Lord, are you going to wash my feet?" Jesus replied, "You do not realize now what I am doing, but later you will understand." "No," said Peter, "you shall never wash my feet." Jesus answered, "Unless I wash you, you have no part with me." "Then, Lord," Simon Peter replied, "not just my feet but my hands and my head as well!" Jesus answered, "Those who have had a bath need only to wash their feet; their whole body is clean. And you are clean, though not every one of you." For he knew who was going to betray him, and that was why he said not every one was clean.

When he had finished washing their feet, he put on his clothes and returned to his place. "Do you understand what I have done for you?" he asked them. "You call me 'Teacher' and 'Lord,' and rightly so, for that is what I am. Now that I, your Lord and Teacher, have washed your feet, you also should wash one another's feet. I have set you an example that you should do as I have done for you. Very truly I tell you, no servant is greater than his master, nor is a messenger greater than the one who sent him. Now that you know these things, you will be blessed if you do them."

(John 13: 2-17, NIV)

This is a pretty familiar story that we may have heard many times. It is one of the best examples that Jesus sets to show how love is not proud, but humble. He was humble enough to voluntarily wash all the disciples' dirty feet and willing to wash one of the most untouchable areas of a person, because of how filthy it can get from trampling through the rocky and dusty streets in open-toed sandals. Not to mention, how weird it is to touch other people's feet, especially if they are not baby's feet. However, I want to put emphasis on how He was so humble that He was willing to even wash the feet of the one who was going to betray Him. By this time, it was already established that the devil put in place what he had planned in Judas, so Jesus was well aware beforehand of Judas's purpose to betray Him. Because Jesus already knew of Judas's plan, He could have been too proud to wash Judas's feet and skipped him, but instead, He included him in the process. Jesus did this because He wanted to show the disciples that while yet one of them was unclean and would remain unclean even after the washing of his feet, He was still willing to include him in this time of being served by His acts of kindness. Jesus was not too proud to include Judas, because He was not trying to show Himself as one with higher importance or higher dignity of superiority over another. Sure, Jesus had a high purpose unlike any other purpose that we have, but He wanted to show that His purpose was not out of vanity, but pure humbleness and love. His purpose was for everyone, and because of His goodness, we all have a chance to accept His love and grace, no matter what we have done or who we are. He humbled Himself for all of us.

When we are too proud, it does not allow us to connect with others or for others to connect with us. When we are too proud, we are blocking others to be able to engage with us in ways that will allow for productive communication, cooperative problem-solving, empathetic reconciliation, or an honest and meaningful relationship. Notice how Jesus responded to Peter when he told Jesus that He will not ever wash his feet. Jesus said that if He did not do so, then Peter would not have any part with Him. He wanted to make sure that by Him being humbled to wash his feet, it symbolized the allowance of Peter to have this clean and purified relationship with Him. Jesus does not want to block us from experiencing His all, so the washing of the feet shows the humiliation needed to have a wonderful and pure relationship with Him.

When we are in a relationship, pride can easily get in the way of having a pure and wonderful relationship. Pride can actually destroy a relationship, because of the unclean thoughts and selfish energy that go into being too proud. When we let our pride get in the way, we are missing out on growing, improving, learning, and receiving. Pride is such a destructive measure and is definitely not from God, but from the enemy. It's the natural born flesh that we have in us. It's used to retaliate against authority, to make ourselves seem more important than others, to oppose righteousness, and to defy closeness. Dealing with a prideful person can be very challenging, because it is hard to see eye to eye with a person who thinks the world should revolve around their needs. But, rest assured that if a person is a believer in Christ, then He will know exactly what is needed to bring them to a humble state, in order to remind them that He is in control of the world, not them.

Reflection Questions:

Question 1: When an issue is brought to your attention by your mate, do you feel like you understand why it is an issue? How do you respond to ensure you understand it? Give an example.

Question 2: When you try to bring up an issue to your mate, do you feel like it is easy to communicate it to them? Why or why not? Does pride get in the way?

Love Does Not Dishonor

"Jesus left Galilee and went to the Jordan River to be baptized by John. But John kept objecting and said, "I ought to be baptized by you. Why have you come to me?"Jesus answered, "For now this is how it should be, because we must do all that God wants us to do." Then John agreed. So Jesus was baptized. And as soon as he came out of the water, the sky opened, and he saw the Spirit of God coming down on him like a dove. Then a voice from heaven said, "This is my own dear Son, and I am pleased with him."

(Matthew 3:13-17, NIV)

"Therefore God exalted him to the highest place and gave him the name that is above every name, that at the name of Jesus every knee should bow, in heaven and on earth and under the earth, and every tongue acknowledge that Jesus Christ is Lord, to the glory of God the Father."

(Philippians 2:9-11, NIV)

The most important thing that Jesus wanted to make sure He did not lack was His profound interest in the glory of God, Abba, His Father. Everything Jesus did, He did it all for the glory of His Father and honored Him. For the people, He was humbled; He carried out miraculous healings and miraculous prosperities; He served others; He taught; and He loved. On the flip side of that, what He did for the glory of God for us was hard, it was a struggle, it was testy, it was long-suffering, it was painfully excruciating, and not what He wanted to do on His own. But, He wanted to honor His Father and He knew it was all for the glory of His Father. He wanted nothing more than to fulfill God's plan, even if it seemed unbearable. Because of this, God was pleased with Him and not only fulfilled His almighty plan, but exalted Jesus to have all power in His hands. If Jesus did not go through with His plan, then He would have been dishonoring the Father.

When you place honor towards someone, it is to show immense admiration, worth, or high regard for them. You show such a respect for them, that dishonoring them would not even be an interest to you. So, when you dishonor someone, what you are doing is showing a disgrace, or shame, towards them. Love makes sure to lift someone up, whether speaking directly to them or about them to someone else. When honoring someone, you respect their needs, attributes, desires, and would want to make sure that you are esteeming them for their value.

When Jesus was nailed in between two thieves, one was honoring Him and the other was dishonoring Him.

"One of the criminals who hung there hurled insults at him: "Aren't you the Messiah? Save yourself and us!"

But the other criminal rebuked him. "Don't you fear God," he said, "since you are under the same sentence? We are punished justly, for we are getting what our deeds deserve. But this man has done nothing wrong."

(Luke 23: 39-40, NIV)

17

The criminal who was dishonoring Jesus was insulting and mocking Him as if He was no one. He was putting Jesus at the same level as he was, which was a criminal. Jesus was King of Kings, the Messiah, the One and only, and he was putting Him down to make Him seem like He was no better than himself. The criminal on the other side of Jesus, however, was honoring Jesus and humbled himself to recognize who Jesus was. He scolded the other criminal for talking about Jesus the way that he did and made sure that he honored Jesus for doing what He was doing, especially when He did not deserve it.

I use this scripture to show how we can easily dishonor someone just to make us feel better about who we are. But, when we honor someone, we recognize people for exactly who they are and are comfortable enough to express it.

Reflection Questions:

Question 1: How do you honor your mate? Give examples.

Question 2: Have you ever felt disgraced by your spouse? If so, how?

Love is Not Self-Seeking

There is no one better to show how love is not self-seeking than Jesus. When Jesus walked amongst the people of the earth, He came to heal, deliver, give hope, peace, happiness, and above all, He came to give self-sacrificing love.

"This is my commandment, that you love one another just as I have loved you. No one has love greater than this, that someone should surrender his life in behalf of his friends."

(John 15: 12-13, ESV)

Every single act Jesus did was to show His love for us. He loved us so much that He took His last breath just for us. His last breath on earth did not stop there. He wanted a personal experience with each of us. Yes, even now. There are billions and billions of people who walk the earth, yet He died just so that He can have a relationship with us. Not just any relationship, but a very personal and meaningful relationship where He takes each of us individually and heals us, delivers us, gives us hope, peace, and joy in the way that He knows we will receive it and embrace it. He did not do anything for Himself, it was all for us.

He does command us to love one another, just as He has loved us, but the truth is that none of us has love greater than His love and without Him as our Lord, we cannot even come close to it. However, the one thing that we can, at the very least, practice is how to love without it being *self-seeking*. In our own natural flesh, we can fall very easily into loving someone based on what we can get out of it. When you love only to self-seek what you can get out of it, then it becomes manipulation, and not genuine. Paul says it best when he says this:

"Love is to be sincere and active [the real thing—without guile and hypocrisy]. Hate what is evil [detest all ungodliness, do not tolerate wickedness]; hold on tightly to what is good. Be devoted to one another with [authentic] brotherly affection [as members of one family], give preference to one another in honor; never lagging behind in diligence; aglow in the Spirit, enthusiastically serving the Lord; constantly rejoicing in hope [because of our confidence in Christ], steadfast and patient in distress, devoted to prayer [continually seeking wisdom, guidance, and strength], contributing to the needs of God's people, pursuing [the practice of] hospitality."

(Romans 12:9-12, AMP)

When we love, it is to be sincere and without guile and hypocrisy. If there is anything we should seek when we love one another, it is wisdom, guidance, and strength to be able to tolerate one another in a loving spirit. Unfortunately, many who get engaged and eventually marry don't always evaluate if their love for one another is genuine. Some of us have fallen in love because of what someone does for us or what they can provide for us. Some of us manipulate to make the other feel like they are being loved and it becomes a long cycle. When we are young, we don't always recognize this, but Paul gives a good statement when it comes to loving sincerely.

When you genuinely love one another, you are not looking to be fulfilled by that person; instead, you are finding ways to fulfill that person. You should be able to look at that person and say, "What can I do to make you happy for the rest of your life?" or "What can I do to ensure that you know that you are loved every day for the rest of your life?"

Reflection Questions:

Question 1: List attributes that your mate has that make you feel genuinely loved.

Question 2: Have there been any actions that would lead you to believe that you are being manipulated to feel like you are being loved?

Question 3: How do you feel like you genuinely love your mate? Does your mate agree or disagree?

Love is Not Easily Angered

There were only a few instances where Jesus displayed the emotion of anger, and one that we are familiar with is when He was in the temple and overturned the tables:

"Jesus entered the temple courts and drove out all who were buying and selling there. He overturned the tables of the money changers and the benches of those selling doves. "It is written," he said to them, "'My house will be called a house of prayer,' but you are making it 'a den of robbers."

(Matthew 21:12-13, NIV)

I can imagine how the disciples felt when Jesus showed this emotion of anger after He had clearly shown grace, mercy, kindness, patience, and other characteristics of love. This was a side of Him that was not displayed prior to this incident, so I'm sure they could all agree that it must have taken so much for Jesus to get to that emotion.

When we think of anger, we think of an outrageous act of red fuming outbursts; an uncontrolled reaction that escalates into vein popping, fist matching, and loud shouts of unkind words. Yes, anger most definitely can get to that point; however, not necessarily. We can show anger towards each other in subtle ways like not speaking to each other and shutting down, giving a cold shoulder and abrupt responses, or avoid being in each other's presence. However we choose to show this emotion, one thing is clear, and that is not to be easily angered. God gave us this emotion, but it is not to be used as a self-seeking manipulating tool to get what we want.

When Jesus showed His emotion of anger, it was for pure motive and to address His genuine concern for sinful behavior and excessive immorality. Jesus is pure and the opposite of immoral, so when He got angry, it was His way of expressing the frustration He had towards those He loved, but were not accepting His invitation to receive it and have faith; the faith to have in Him for their needs. Instead, they were in a place of worship and prayer, and using it for their own advantages, for their own riches. He was not easily angered because it was a concern many years prior and God knew all along that the temple was being used as a den of robbers. He did not get angry because of selfish driven direction or to manipulate fear into those He was trying to address. He also did not prolong His anger. He addressed the matter and handled it. He did not hold resentful feelings bottled in or bitterness towards who He was addressing He simply got it out at the proper time and made an effective statement.

There is nothing wrong with getting angry when needed, but just make sure that it is for the right reasons and that you do not let angry emotions build up in your heart. If you do, then it can cause you to be easily angered in everything else and cause you to hurt others in a dishonoring way. When there are issues in a relationship, it is best to address them right away in a loving manner to one another. If your mate gets easily angered and it leads to an unpredictable outburst of rage that can also become physical, then please re-evaluate what you are getting into. Most people, who stay in a relationship with someone who is easily angered, continue to stay because they have hopes that they will change for the sake of love. However, please identify that this type of anger is definitely not the love that Jesus shows.

Reflection Questions:

Question 1: What are some things that you feel you get easily angry about? What is the driving factor of why you get easily angered about it?

Question 2: Do you feel like some of the things that your mate is easily angered about is driven towards you or their own selfish inner problems?

Love Keeps No Record of Wrongs

In our own human nature, it is hard not to keep tally marks when a person has wronged us, especially when they are repeat offenders. After a while, you can become bitter and resent a person who keeps doing wrong against you. But, according to Scripture, love does not keep record of wrongs. Of course, the ultimate example of how no wrongs are kept is when Jesus was hanging so tiredly on the cross and said, "Forgive them for, they know not what they do." (Luke 23:34, ESV) Who was He referring to? He was not only referring to the very people who put them up there, but He was referring to all of us. Those of us who have not yet come to know Him.

"You see, at just the right time, when we were still powerless, Christ died for the ungodly. Very rarely will anyone die for a righteous person, though for a good person someone might possibly dare to die. But God demonstrates his own love for us in this: While we were still sinners, Christ died for us."

(Romans 5:6-8, NIV)

When we were doing our own thing, making our own decisions for our own selfish gain, we did not realize that we were sinning against God's desires for us. We each can look back on our lives and start to point out the mistakes we made because we did not know any better, as sinners. Yet, even as far back as you can remember, Jesus still never kept tally marks on all your wrongdoings. In fact, it is because of our sins yesterday, today, and tomorrow that He wanted to complete His mission. What a huge example of how *love keeps no records of wrong*. When we keep records of wrongs, not only are we keeping ourselves into bondage of how unfair things are to us, but we are also keeping the other person in bondage of their mistakes. Keeping wrongs of your mate will not allow you to move forward in a relationship in a healthy state of mind, because you are focusing so much on all the past mistakes. This is not to say that you should not address when someone has wronged you. Naturally, you should always address the wrong against you. Hopefully, after addressing the wrong, you both can come to an end result of repentance, forgiveness, and resolution. If so, then it should not be brought up again as a reminder to consistently beat them up. Yes, there is a chance that whatever wrong that happened against you may happen again, but if this is true, then it is something that you need to evaluate and decide if it could be something that is worth forgiving again, until it is made right. If how they wronged you seemed like it was too much to bear to begin with, then utilize this time of engagement to really buckle down on what you can stand to live with before you get married. Because, there is no doubt that there will be some mistakes that will be made against you and it will hurt. If grace is not what you know how to give, then marriage will definitely teach you how to give grace to your spouse.

Reflection Questions:

Question 1: Has your mate done something to you that you felt was very wrong? What was it and how did you deal with it? Are you constantly reminded of it? Do you think you can forgive them if they did it again and maybe even another time against you?

Question 2: When you have done something wrong against your mate, what are the chances of you not doing it again (be honest)? Why or why not?

Question 3: If your mate wronged you in the same manner that you wronged them, how would you handle it? Would you be able to forgive them if they did it to you several times?

Love Does Not Delight in Evil but Rejoices with the Truth

"Jesus answered, "I am the way and the truth and the life. No one comes to the Father except through me."

(John 14:6, NIV)

Jesus did not have to set an example of truth, He is Truth. It is so exciting that we can rejoice in the truth that Jesus is the way, the truth, and the life. That is exceptionally good news! For many of us who are in Christ, we can truly understand what this means to us personally. So, rejoicing in this truth is life changing. The reason why it is life changing is because God completely knows the depths of our hearts and He delights in our good qualities and not our immoral and evil habits. It is not to say that God dismisses us for our sins, but because of His love to us and for us, it encourages us to want to sin no more. It's His love that we can rejoice about, because He does not want us to stay as evil little doers. He rejoices when we come to Him and want to turn away from the worldly desires of this earth.

The father of the prodigal son is a parable of how God rejoices in truth and not evil.

"When he came to his senses, he said, 'How many of my father's hired servants have food to spare, and here I am starving to death! I will set out and go back to my father and say to him: Father, I have sinned against heaven and against you. I am no longer worthy to be called your son; make me like one of your hired servants.' So he got up and went to his father.

24

"But while he was still a long way off, his father saw him and was filled with compassion for him; he ran to his son, threw his arms around him and kissed him."

"The son said to him, 'Father, I have sinned against heaven and against you. I am no longer worthy to be called your son.'

"But the father said to his servants, 'Quick! Bring the best robe and put it on him. Put a ring on his finger and sandals on his feet. Bring the fattened calf and kill it. Let's have a feast and celebrate. For this son of mine was dead and is alive again; he was lost and is found.' So they began to celebrate."

(Luke 15:17-24, NIV)

Out of the two sons this father had, this son deliberately took his father's inheritance that was gifted to him and wasted it on evil things. He used it and lived his life lavishly and wildly, until he had nothing left to spend and eventually ended up in famine. When he realized his own foolishness, he decided to go back to his father. Now, his father could have very well delighted in evil by throwing it in his son's face and letting him know that he got what he deserved. His father could have laughed at him and told him that he was indeed a fool and sent him back to where he came from. His father could have told him that he had to work like one of his servants and twice as hard, since he wasted all the money that was given to him. However, his father did the opposite and rejoiced. Instead of him delighting in throwing his son's evil doings in his face, he celebrated the fact that his son had come back and not only came back, but confessed the truth of his sin. This father rejoiced with love and not evil backlash.

It can be very hard when someone close to you has done wrong against you, as mentioned earlier. At times, we want to see something bad happen to them as pay back and get into this mindset of, "God bless them." Meaning, God curse them. But, that is not loving them with truth. When we see our mates through grace and mercy, we tend not to want to curse them, but love them in such a way that God loves us. We don't want to seek revenge or show some kind of retaliation towards them. We should be able to be open and honest towards one another, in order to love in truth. If your relationship is not built on truth and honesty, then you will be living a life on eggshells. You should not have to live a life where you can't be true to who you are or a life where you can't speak truth to someone else because of fear. As a couple, you should be able to share honest feelings and hold each other accountable for each other's actions, in order to grow a strong relationship without judgment.

Reflection Questions:

Question 1: When your mate does something against you, but repents. Do you throw it in their face and retaliate in some way towards them or do you accept the apology and move forward? Does your mate agree with your answer?

Love Always Protects

"I pray for them. I am not praying for the world, but for those you have given me, for they are yours. All I have is yours, and all you have is mine. And glory has come to me through them. I will remain in the world no longer, but they are still in the world, and I am coming to you. Holy Father, protect them by the power of your name, the name you gave me, so that they may be one as we are one. While I was with them, I protected them and kept them safe by that name you gave me. None has been lost except the one doomed to destruction so that Scripture would be fulfilled."

(John 17:9-12, NIV)

Praying for someone is one of the greatest forms of protection that we can ever receive. Jesus made it very clear in this prayer that He wanted to keep those that He loved, protected. Protected from what? He wanted His believers who were following Him to be protected from the world that was against them, so that they will reach oneness with Him. He wanted to make sure He protects all of us from the exposure of false teachings, damage from sin, and destruction that Satan will try and throw to kill, rob, and destroy. While Jesus was on earth, He protected those who followed Him, so that they would keep their eyes on Him. But, because He was leaving the world, He also wanted to make sure that they were protected once He was gone. There was more to come for them while Jesus was gone, so Jesus was ensuring they were protected with the full armor of God, and that we have refuge in Him. Not only refuge in Him, but He sent the Holy Spirit to help protect us, as well. The Holy Spirit guides us, comforts us, counsels us, intercedes for us, and strengthens us in our time of need as a form of protecting us.

Love is very protective. We see it when mama becomes a mama bear for her cubs, or when a husband stresses the importance of a shot gun for his daughter's boyfriend, or when a husband voluntarily gives up his warm coat for his cold wife. There are many ways that we can see how we protect one another. We should be available however we can to be a form of protection for those we love. As a couple, you will have to be prepared for the attacks that will come up against you when you are married; the attacks from the world and the attacks by each other. However, there will be times when you may not physically or mentally be available to protect each other. That is when prayer is used to protect when we cannot see what is going on. Love is always willing to go out of our way to protect those we love, but love is always willing to pray over them, too. With so much that can come up against you, especially the institution of marriage, protecting one another is vital.

Reflection Questions:

Question 1: Do you feel like your mate protects you (protects you emotionally, spiritually, and physically)? Why or why not?

Question 2: What do you feel like you would need to protect your mate from the most today or in the future?

Love Always Trusts

"Trust in the LORD with all your heart and lean not on your own understanding; in all your ways submit to him, and he will make your paths straight."

(Proverbs 3:5-6, NIV)

God wants us to trust Him in everything, but mostly to trust who He is. He is God almighty. He is perfect, all knowing, all present, all giving, all good, and all love. There is absolutely nothing about Him that you can't trust. He will never do anything to hurt you, abandon you, or violate you. He sent His only begotten Son, Jesus to die for us, so that we can have access to Him and His ways. So, for us, that means we should trust Him with all of our heart, no matter if it is the good or the bad. He knows exactly what to do with our heart when we share it with Him.

With that being said, we cannot always trust in human beings because humans can hurt us, abandon us, and violate us. Since human beings are not perfect and have fleshly desires, there is always possibility that they will do something that is not trustworthy. However, when it says love always trusts what that means is that we should not fill our days wondering whether or not our mates should be trusted. We have already established that humans are not always to be trusted, but we cannot consume ourselves and just believe that they are going to do something that will hurt us. I know you are probably thinking, "Well, I am just preparing myself in case they do hurt me." Remember, love does not expect the worse. Love expects the best, and if for whatever reason you cannot love someone enough to trust them, then maybe you need to evaluate why you can't trust them or evaluate why you have trust issues. Love always expects the possibilities of a great relationship, so when you are constantly in distrust of your mate, then you are doubting they are good for you.

What if they did something against you that was not trustworthy? If this is the case, and you are not married yet, then this is the time when you can come to terms on whether or not what they did against you is worth working past or not. If you decide that it is worth working past, then that is when you are expecting a better outcome. In this case, in order to show that love always trust, then you lift it up to trust God with all your heart. If you were wronged because of something your mate did, bring it to God and trust Him to show you whether or not you can deal with it. The rest is up to your mate on what they do to show that they are trustworthy again. If your mate is doing everything they can to rebuild trust in a healthy manner, then God knows the outcome of everything and He will move in your heart to trust or to let go. But, until you get an answer, don't let it consume you.

Reflection Questions:

Question 1: Has your mate done anything that violated the trust in your relationship? How are you dealing with it?

Question 2: Have you done anything that violated trust in your relationship? If so, what are you doing or what can you do to ensure that you are trustworthy again?

Question 3: If God were to come and sit down right next to you and ask you if you trusted Him, would you be able to say that you completely do? Explain why or why not?

Love Always Hopes

"Paul, an apostle of Christ Jesus by the command of God our Savior and of Christ Jesus our hope."

(I Timothy 1, NIV)

If you have not discovered already, then now is a good time to understand that Jesus is our hope. When our Heavenly Father saw that the Mosaic Law was too hard for His people to keep, He knew that eventually, He had to send His Son. He needed His Son Jesus to come, because the law was there to keep the people safe and holy, but because of the sinful nature, it was impossible to keep such a law and reap the benefits for doing so. But, because God loved His people so much, He sent the Messiah as the hope for the new nations. He always wanted His people to follow the laws He laid down for them, because His laws were perfect and the best way to live, but it was the people who were not perfect and continued to fail to live by the laws. So, Jesus came to give us all hope and a better life.

Hope always expects a desired fulfillment for an outcome. When we hope, we are anticipating that all will work out well and that we can see the light at the end of the tunnel. So, when Scripture says love always hopes, then the love we have for one another in our relationships always hopes for the best in everything.

When you are in a relationship, you are two imperfect people that have different philosophies, different perspectives, different techniques, and different personalities. Some of the differences may be better than the other's differences, but it really depends on which side of the spectrum you are on. What I mean by that, is because of the differences, one person will always believe that their way is the perfect way and the other partner's way may not be. But, one thing is clear that when you are looking through two different lenses, then the best thing to do is align it with God's Word and decide which one is closest to it. If the other's is way off, then that is where hope comes in. You know where the differences are, but you hope that they will align with the lens that God looks through. Jesus is our source of hope and when we look to Him, then we believe that all things will work out for the good; even in our relationships. Without hope, then there is nothing to look forward to in the relationship. If you are unable to hope and expect a fulfilling outcome in the person or relationship you are in, then it will be hard to grow with them.

Reflection Questions:

Question 1: What differences in your mate do you hope to see improve in your relationship? Why is it so important to you to see improvement in those differences? Does it align with God?

Question 2: What is the most important accomplishment that you hope will happen after you get married? How hard or easy do you think it will be to obtain and why?

Love Always Perseveres

"Consider him who endured such opposition from sinners, so that you will not grow weary and lose heart."

(Hebrews 12:3, NIV)

Jesus went through a great deal specifically just for you and not only a great deal by the people who hated Him, but those who also claimed to love Him. He was rejected by Jewish leaders, because of His Truth. His disciples fell into temptation to sleep when He asked them to keep watch, while He prayed in the Garden of Gethsemane. He was betrayed by Judas when he gave up His whereabouts for money. He was abandoned by all His disciples when the soldiers came to take Jesus. He was denied by Peter when asked if he knew Jesus. He carried the burden of our sins during His long journey to the cross. He was abused by the Roman guards. He was shamed by being crucified in between two thieves, while He was nothing but innocent. Lastly, His heart stopped beating and His side, closest to His heart, was pierced to show His death. Temptation, betrayal, denial, abandonment, burden, rejection, shame, abuse, and heartbreak were all the things Jesus experienced, because of His interest in us all. It is hard to imagine how He felt going through what He had to endure, yet still willing to accomplish His Father's will and purpose. He did not ask for any of this to be brought unto Him, but He knew there was purpose behind it. He could have, at any point, backed out and given up, but He pressed on because He was not going to let Satan take what was His. He persevered with great focus and all because He loved you.

When love perseveres, it is steadfast and is determined to walk it out no matter what obstacles of hurdles, storms, or blocks come up. Our relationships may suffer any one, or several, of the same emotions that Jesus suffered. Not to the same extent, but in the same manner. Temptation, betrayal, denial, abandonment, burden, rejection, shame, abuse, and heartbreak can take place at any time in our marriage, but the question is how willing are you to endure these emotions and follow through with the end purpose of your relationship? Yes, it can be excruciating and seem unbearable, and even unfair, but how determined are you to make sure that you will do all that you can do and put all your faith in the one who created marriage, so that He can reveal His purpose for it? That is a hard question to answer, isn't it? None of us want to go through any circumstance that can create excruciating emotions, because we are not expecting our hearts to break into pieces, especially not for the expense of others. I'm not trying to discourage you from marriage, but these are emotions that you may or may not face in the future once you are committed to your vows. So, will you be able to persevere through such actions?

Reflection Questions:

Question 1: What do you think would be the hardest circumstance if you were married to persevere through? Really think about this question and then decide if you think you could persevere through it as a couple.

Question 2: What would be the one thing that you know in your heart you would not want to persevere through?

You will find that this is one of the longest chapters of the book. The emphasis of God's definition of *love* is imperative to know, because if these characteristics are not genuine and sincere towards each other, then ask yourself what kind of love is it that you have for one another? It's is not to say that who you are thinking about marrying has to have perfection in this kind of love, but it is a guideline that will help you see which characteristics of love your mate has and which ones need to be paid especially careful of if they do not have them, that can eventually hurt your relationship. You have heard the expression, "love conquers all," and many of us believe that as long as there is love, then you can get through anything. But, the truth is, if you do not have this kind of love that God clearly defines, then love may not be enough. To have a Godly kind of love will help you get through your marriage, so that you can handle the best times and the worst times. In addition to this kind of love, there are pre-obstacles and preparations that need to be observed, while you are engaged to be married. So, pay close attention to the next chapters, because they can guide you to what is true and what's real. This book is not to discourage you, but to encourage you to go into a lasting relationship *eyes wide open*. As you read through the chapters, answer the questions with each other in ALL honesty with nothing holding you back. Because, the first thing that should be established in your relationship is on the basis of complete truth and not half-truths. Be blessed!

Reflection Questions:

Question 1: What kind of love do you think you have for your mate? Examples: puppy love, high school sweetheart love, lustful love, romantic love, psychotic love, godly-wisdom love, crazy-stupid love, etc.? Do you feel like it aligns with God's definition of love?

Question 2: Based on the breakdown of what love is biblically, which ones stand out most in your mate?

Chapter 2

Against our Roles

"So God created mankind in his own image,
in the image of God he created them;
male and female he created them."

(Genesis 1:27, NIV)

*F*or centuries, it has been instilled in us about the differences between what girls and boys do. Girls are given baby dolls, so that they can care for and nurture them, kitchen sets, so that they can pretend to go grocery shopping and cook meals, tea sets to entertain the imaginary guest, dress up costumes to imagine being princesses, brides, and ballroom guests, Barbie and Ken dolls in a dream house, so they can venture in a world of husband and wife, coloring books and crafts to be artsy and creative, fake vacuums and brooms to tidy up their homes made out of blankets and sheets, and other things that eventually mold girls to later become the actual role of what they have imagined for years. Boys are given a car collection of the hottest cars that they crash into each other, superhero figurines and costumes to kill and destroy the bad people, cops and robber sets to be hard workers in keeping the streets safe, tools to fix things in their imaginary work station, Lego sets to build cities and spaceships, and other things that later mold them to become the actual role of what they imagined for years.

Key phrase: Things that later mold them to become the actual role of what they imagined for years.

Girls have been given everything they need to understand the roles of being a domestic engineer, and boys have been given everything they need to understand the roles of being *Mr. Protect* and fix things by your own powerful strength. We don't generally give boys baby dolls, so that they can learn how to be good fathers or a kitchen set, so that they can understand how to cook for their family, or tuxedo costumes, so they can imagine getting married or be the prince charming waiting to pick up Cinderella in a gentleman way. We don't generally give girls pretend guns to protect the streets, plastic wrenches and screw drivers to fix things around the house, or a Superman costume, so they can pretend to leap over a two-story building. Each gender is exposed and is given everything that naturally prepares them for those years of experience of what they will eventually become in their own homes. So, while the girls are practicing being homemakers, the boys are practicing being providers and protectors.

Is there anything wrong with that? No, it is our normal world and has been for centuries, and it is a part of our résumé of role experiences. It's initially a great experience for us as children. As we become a little older, we start to see the roles with a little more depth. We see it in our own homes, we see it through societal interactions with other people, and we can also see it through media. However, media has taken such a turn on role definitions that it can cause confusion. Men can carry themselves as jackasses and do foolish things, or as bachelors having more than one relationship at a time. Women can be viewed as high sexually-charged homewreckers, or *Ms. Independent* who does not need anyone but herself. What is also more prevalent are men and women who view homosexuality or transgender as today's norm and something that God must have created. But, for the sake of the typical stereotype, we will simply stress the norm of the boy and girl experiences we started off with in this chapter.

At some point, we start to formulate our past experiences with our own idea of what we should be as man and woman and add it to our résumé of role experiences. So, by the time we get married, we have this blueprint of what our own role experiences should look like. Still not a problem, but will become one when we do not understand the role experiences that have been building up on our spouse's résumé, and therefore we try to project our ideas on them and what we believe they should be. That is like saying to a person who has experience being a doctor, to go fly a plane like a pilot. The doctor will not have pilot experience, because being a doctor is all that they know how to do exceedingly well. But, if the doctor wanted to, then he or she can receive the knowledge to learn how to fly a plane like a pilot. They have to be willing to gain that experience and be willing to take the time to practice. So, in our relationships, we have to come to understand our mate's résumé of role experience. Some of their experience will become very useful and beneficial to accomplish the goals we have for our marriages, but some of them may need some wisdom to help enhance their idea of their role experiences.

Something else to keep in mind, God put some of His attributes in a man to spiritually be who he is and He put some of His attributes in a woman to spiritually be how she is designed. God has both male and female attributes and He delegated what parts of those, in His own image, He wanted the male to have and what the woman to have. He delegated the attributes that He wanted in us, so that the accomplishment of oneness can be obtained in a marriage. Think about that for a minute. Let's go deeper behind that meaning. He delegated His attributes for man to have the likeness of God's male attributes and then for woman to have the likeness of God's female attributes. We are male and female who are distinct from each other, but we have the likeness of God's image in us. So, when we marry, the female and the male attributes that God gave us unite to become one flesh. One flesh in whom? One flesh to come together, so that you are one in Him.

When you become one flesh, the male attributes and the female attributes in the image of God become one complete image in the likeness of God. Isn't that amazing? What else does that remind you of? Yes, the Trinity. God is one and only one, but He exists in three persons; The Father, the Son, and the Holy Spirit. Each of them acts distinctly, but in unity. Even though He is three persons, all three is one equally and eternally, and all three are worthy to be worshipped and praised constitutionally. They each have their purpose, but the purpose is ultimately coming from one and that is God who IS and always will BE.

With this same concept, we can apply it to our roles when it comes to marriage. Even though He delegated His attributes differently in male and female, we are still equal in God's eyes and He expects us to carry our roles as husband and wife distinctly, but equally, so that the accomplishment of oneness can take place in such a way, that you know it is only God. The role as husband and wife that God instructs us to be is wisdom that we have to gain and not something that we automatically learn. Boys are not exactly given toys to show how to be spiritual leaders and how to love their wives like Christ loves the church and girls are not given toys to show how to love their husbands as unto the Lord. These principles were not always instilled in us while we were children. It is wisdom that we willingly have to gain if we want to live our roles under God's design for marriage. Just like the doctor, who, if he wanted to learn to fly a plane, he would have to be willing to gain the knowledge to achieve it. So, the men and women that we have become through role experiences has the ability to become the roles that God designed for us to have successful marriages through the attributes that He has delegated within us. Do not skip to simply your role, because I lay out information about the roles of husbands and wives that can be received by both of you in each section. The purpose is to see how the unity of marriage is also a *trinity*.

Husband's Role

The super-heroes coming to the rescue to destroy the bad people, the plastic tools to fix things that are broken in the imaginary work station, the cop badges to show their job to protect and serve the community. These experiences shape boys to protect, provide, and fix things. These experiences are what bring innate desires to be able to push themselves to seek great careers, so they can provide for their families. These experiences give them the desire to be the heroes to protect their families. These experiences also give them the desire to fix things, both physically in the home and psychologically with people. However, if they are not careful, their ability to try and fix things can turn out disastrous if they attempt to tackle something they have no experience in.   But, on a more serious note, these attributes they have are also a part of how God designed them.

"The LORD God took the man and put him in the Garden of Eden to work it and take care of it. And the LORD God commanded the man, "You are free to eat from any tree in the garden; but you must not eat from the tree of the knowledge of good and evil, for when you eat from it you will certainly die."

(Genesis 2:15-17, NIV)

To Provide and Cultivate

After God finished His works creating the Garden of Eden, He created Adam. He did not waste any time and immediately put Adam to work the grounds of the garden. So, from the beginning of time, man was created to work. Adam was placed in the Garden of Eden and was given a special assignment to care for what God provided for him to live in. Adam was not put in the Garden of Eden to just wander around it and admire its beauty; he was put in it to work. He was to identify what was before him, cultivate, nurture, and promote growth for everything that was in his presence. In addition to his assignment to work, he was able to reap the benefits that came from it.

Work today for men is not exactly the same work that Adam was assigned to, and it is not easily given to them as it was for Adam. Not to discredit Adams work, but it does not compare to the kinds of jobs that are available today. Husbands today have so much that they have to fight up against, as a working man. It begins with just trying to gain the knowledge they need to get a good job, whether it is going through college or just climbing the ladders with experience. Once they get a job, they have to deal with the politics of the atmosphere, personalities, the loads, the temptations, the competition, and so forth. Yet, even though a workplace can possibly become a less pleasurable place to be, it is still a requirement for a man to provide.

Husbands' goals are to make sure that they are able to provide for their family in hopes that they can provide everything needed and more. It is good for husbands who want to provide for their families. God honors a working man who is providing, but if they are not careful, they can get caught up in what the world expects of them to be as providers. The world says make more and more money, so that you can have the bigger homes, the more expensive cars, the vacations to private islands, the higher paying jobs, the higher positions, etc. There is nothing wrong with desiring these things, but you don't have to over-exert yourself to the point where you are not in peace to be able to find joy in these things. For some husbands, working for higher goals may just bring them to a state where their job becomes their priority over their family. To them, all they are thinking about is being able to provide more.

Yes, God does expect you to work and He does want you to provide, but not at the cost of losing your relationship with Him or losing your family. Instead of relying on your self-efforts to be a good provider, rely on God. Everything that you have to be a provider, God gave to you. In the Garden of Eden, Adam had an assignment. His assignment, specifically, was to care for the grounds and name the living creatures. God gave him the mind and the strength to be able to accomplish his assignment. You can imagine that Adam enjoyed his line of work and probably diligently worked, so that he could please God for blessing him with his ability to work. Everything was already provided for Adam to live in and all he had to do was trust God for it and care for it. Likewise, God already provided everything you need to provide, all you have to do is carefully work in trusting God for it. You do not have to work so hard where you are putting it first before everything, especially not before God. Even though Adam had to work, God did not want him to work so hard where it would take the focus off of Him or the focus off of what God was blessing him with next.

"Now the LORD God had formed out of the ground all the wild animals and all the birds in the sky. He brought them to the man to see what he would name them; and whatever the man called each living creature, that was its name. So the man gave names to all the livestock, the birds in the sky and all the wild animals.

But for Adam no suitable helper was found. So the LORD God caused the man to fall into a deep sleep; and while he was sleeping, he took one of the man's ribs and then closed up the place with flesh. Then the

LORD God made a woman from the rib he had taken out of the man, and he brought her to the man."

(Genesis 2:19-22, NIV)

Even Adam had to rest from his line of work. Not only rest from work, but God wanted to provide someone for him, so that she could be a helper to him. A helper who could help be a part of his life and enjoy everything that God provided for them. God put Adam to rest so that when he woke up, He would be revived and able to focus on this woman as a precious gift to him and enjoy her presence. God brought Adam this gift and God made them both rulers over the earth together.

"Then God said, "Let us make mankind in our image, in our likeness, so that they may rule over the fish in the sea and the birds in the sky, over the livestock and all the wild animals, and over all the creatures that move along the ground."

So God created mankind in his own image, in the image of God he created them; male and female he created them.

God blessed them and said to them, "Be fruitful and increase in number; fill the earth and subdue it. Rule over the fish in the sea and the birds in the sky and over every living creature that moves on the ground."

(Genesis 1:26-28, NIV)

God made Adam the primary worker, but He also brought in someone to help him. Not just anyone; He brought a woman who was appealing to him and there to share life with him. He could have brought in another man who had the same exact strength and knowledge as him, but instead, God brought a woman who had a different kind of strength and knowledge to help him. Adam would not have been able to see this woman that God brought to him if he was too busy working in the Garden. If Adam was focused on his job

41

and consumed himself with his assignment, then he would have missed out on his gift.

God does expect you to work and provide, and He honors you for doing so, wherever you are currently in your career. The work He gave you is a blessing, but He also wants to bless you with a helper, a woman, who can be by your side and share all that you will accomplish. You may be thinking that you have to live to work, but God says, no, you live for Him. You work to provide, but don't let your career rule you, or you will not be able to enjoy what God has blessed you with.

"But those who won't care for their relatives, especially those in their own household, have denied the true faith. Such people are worse than unbelievers."

(I Timothy 5:8, NIV)

Being a provider does not just mean to work. It means to be able to provide everything that is needed to care for your household. Not just for the obvious needs like, shelter, food, and clothing, but also the needs for survival, in case of future circumstances like healthcare for illness, life insurance for death, insurance for unforeseen disasters to material things, and 401K or similar for retirement. In addition to these, he expects provisions emotionally and spiritually. We live in a world where unfortunate circumstances can happen at any time, and because of that, we should have something in place to be able to provide what we need to handle them. God instructs provision in order to care for relatives and especially the immediate household and if you do not care to do this, then you are denying your faith in Him. He also goes on to say that if you don't provide, then you are worse than an unbeliever. That is a pretty strong statement to be compared to being worse than an unbeliever. What is an unbeliever? In simple terms, an unbeliever rejects Jesus as their Savior. But, to give you more depth of why not providing is worse than an unbeliever; take a look at a few of the things the Bible says about unbelievers.

"They are darkened in their understanding, alienated from the life of God because of the ignorance that is in them, due to their hardness of heart."

(Ephesians 4:18, NIV)

"But as for the cowardly, the faithless, the detestable, as for murderers, the sexually immoral, sorcerers, idolaters, and all liars, their portion will be in the lake that burns with fire and sulfur, which is the second death."

(Revelation 21:8, NIV)

"The LORD will not allow a righteous person to starve, but he intentionally ignores the desires of a wicked person."

(Proverbs 10:3, NIV)

These are just a few scriptures of what an unbeliever's destiny looks like. To be an unbeliever means that you are separated from God, filled in your own darkness, and will have your desires ignored. This means that you will not be able to fully rejoice in all that He has for you in this life or in the life in His kingdom. So, for the scripture to say if you do not care to provide for your family, then you are worse than an unbeliever; which means that even an unbeliever takes better care of their family than someone who does not care to provide. Why is that so? Why does an unbeliever take care of his family better than someone who is a believer and does not care to provide? Just like God takes care of the birds, which do not worry about how they will eat, God still provides to the unbeliever what they need, but an unbeliever does not have access to what God wants to truly bless them with. If you are a believer in Christ, then you know that Jesus died on the cross for your sins to be forgiven, so that you can live life more abundantly, and live eternally in Heaven. You have access to an all powerful, all knowing God who wants to provide any and everything for you to be able to, in turn, provide for your family in every way and in all things. All you have to do is ask for it and trust Him that it will be given to you. God has everything you need to make sure your family is taken care of financially, emotionally, and spiritually, and He wants to give you the best for your family. It is because of

43

your faith in Him that you will receive all that you need to provide and more. So, if you are a believer and you choose not to want to provide for your family, then you are worse than an unbeliever, because you are denying what God has already done for you to be able to provide. An unbeliever denies Jesus because they do not know or want to believe, but a believer knows and if they choose not to provide, then they are denying the faith of what Jesus died on the cross for them to have.

God designed you to be a great provider for your home and there is surely nothing wrong with asking Him to provide everything that your family needs and more. He knows your motives for wanting what you ask of and is willing to give you everything that is pure in motive. This is not to say that the woman you choose to be with must not be part of providing, Because when God joined them together, He told them both to rule over the earth, which means as a couple, you should come into agreement of how you want to share the responsibility of being a provider financially, spiritually, and emotionally.

You should also provide a healthy emotional atmosphere for the love of your life. God made woman so uniquely and she is to be a part of you in everything. She is your lot in life. Don't let providing financially cause you to lose your enjoyment or your focus on her.

"Enjoy life with your wife, whom you love, all the days of this meaningless life that God has given you under the sun—all your meaningless days. For this is your lot in life and in your toilsome labor under the sun."

(Ecclesiastes 9:9, NIV)

Okay, this scripture seems a bit brutal, but what God is basically saying in a nutshell, is that the life God provided for you and the days you live in is meaningless without your soon-to-be-wife. She is the lot of your life; the reason for your existence, the total being of whom you should focus on to help you get through the toilsome labor you have been passed on by Adam. According to God, you are living a meaningless life, but it is the wife that you should enjoy to make it meaningful. I promise you I did not manipulate this scripture, it is verbatim. Your bride will want nothing more than for you to delight in her and provide a healthy, emotional, and stable environment for her. When you provide this for her, then in turn, it brings enjoyment to your life. You are going to want your bride-to-be that rock; that cheerleader; that *ride or die chick* to help you get through your difficult times. However, when you do not enjoy being with your bride, she cannot be any of that for you, because she will feel devalued. If your bride feels devalued, then it will be very difficult for her to give value to you. The more value you put into her, the more your life can become of value, as a married couple.

Enjoying your bride means spending time with her intellectually, spiritually, and physically. Enjoy everything about her and who she is. Enjoy doing things with her and for her. Enjoy everything in your life that pertains to her, period. You will be putting her well-being above all earthly things, and she will receive it with gratitude and want more than anything to treat you like the king you are, so that you, too, will have a meaningful existence.

Why is this important? Well, in the next chapter, you will focus on how your bride is to be *Holy-Spirit like*. You are to be *Christ-like* in the holy-matrimony of marriage, and she is to be *Holy-Spirit like*. But for now, I wanted to point out why it is so important to enjoy your wife and lift her up, because if you don't, then you will be quenching her role as your *helper*. The best way to explain this is to show you what happens when we quench the Holy Spirit within us and correlate it to how quenching your bride-to-be can affect her in the same manner.

"Do not quench [subdue, or be unresponsive to the working and guidance of] the [Holy] Spirit. Do not scorn or reject gifts of prophecy or prophecies [spoken revelations—words of instruction or exhortation or warning]. But test all things carefully [so you can recognize what is good]. Hold firmly to that which is good."

(1 Thessalonians 5:19-21, AMP)

45

We already know that when Jesus said He had to go away so that the Helper will come, He was referring to the *Holy Spirit*. The Holy Spirit is an amazing gift to us, because He guides, encourages, comforts, and gives us discernment. However, in order to really be in tune with Holy Spirit, we have to commune with Him at all times of the day. If we do not and decide to ignore, or be unresponsive to Holy Spirit, then we miss out on the significance of Him within us. We begin to grieve Holy Spirit, causing un-fulfillment of who we are in Christ. Everything we do becomes hard self-effort and not Spirit-led. Our existence becomes cloudy and uncertain when we do not rely on Holy Spirit to help us live.

If your bride-to-be is your helper, then in the same manner, you could grieve her when you do not commune with her, enjoy her, and lift her up. Finding a wife is good and remember, she is a gift that was given to you. She is there to help guide you in the direction you are to both take through life, comfort you when things are not at its best, encourage you in your leadership role, and help discern what will be right and wrong throughout your journey together. If you choose to ignore her or lack communion with her, then she, too, will not be able to be the best in her role as a wife to you. You need her to be at her best, so you two can walk throughout life together with complete matrimony purpose.

Reflection Questions:

Question 1: What are your views on being the sole provider for the household?

Question 2: Do you believe that your bride-to-be is a gift sent to you? Why?

To Protect

"Greater love has no one than this: to lay down one's life for one's friends."

(John 15:13, NIV)

Men have this natural desire to protect; to be the *Superman* who takes a bullet for their Lois Lane, or the *Spiderman* who swings through buildings to catch their Gwen Stacy. Well, maybe they believed that in child's play, but God did design them to have greater strength. So, with this God-given attribute, it is required of you to protect your bride, so that she feels secure. Surely, you would not ask her to get out and push the car, while you steer to get out of the mud or ask her to get geared up, so she can check out the sound of a broken window downstairs for burglars. Showing that you are willing to lay down your life for her, shows greater love. Besides the obvious kind of protection, men, you are also to protect her emotionally and spiritually.

When God made Adam, He put him to work and then gave him specific instructions:

"You are free to eat from any tree in the garden; [17] *but you must not eat from the tree of the knowledge of good and evil, for when you eat from it you will certainly die."*

(Genesis 1:16-17, NIV)

God gave him these instructions alone, so that he would clearly understand his responsibilities and the importance of accountability if he was disobedient. God clearly said, here is my garden I provided to you; you must work to care for it and you are welcome to eat anything from it, except the tree of the knowledge of good and evil, or you will die if you disobey my command. It could not have been made any clearer than that. Then, from Adam's rib, God brought a woman to share the beauty of the Garden. She was made from the side of his rib, which signifies being under his wing, or arm, to keep safe and protect under the same instructions.

"The man said, "This is now bone of my bones and flesh of my flesh; she shall be called 'woman,' for she was taken out of man."

(Genesis 2:23, NIV)

47

This scripture foreshadows God's instruction for husbands to protect then and God's instruction to protect now in the New Testament.

"So ought men to love their wives as their own bodies. He that loveth his wife loveth himself.

For no man ever yet hated his own flesh; but nourisheth and cherisheth it, even as the Lord the church:"

(Ephesians 5:28-29, KJV)

At some point, Adam must have given Eve instructions not to eat from the tree, because she was familiar with reciting it when the serpent approached her. However, either Adam did not relay it to her verbatim of God's instruction or she did not quite hear it correctly. Whatever the reason, the serpent was able to deceive her into the temptation, because she did not have the instruction written clearly in her heart to be able to rebuke the serpent.

"Now the serpent was more crafty than any of the wild animals the LORD *God had made. He said to the woman, "Did God really say, 'You must not eat from any tree in the garden'?"*

The woman said to the serpent, "We may eat fruit from the trees in the garden, but God did say, 'You must not eat fruit from the tree that is in the middle of the garden, and you must not touch it, or you will die.'"

"You will not certainly die," the serpent said to the woman. "For God knows that when you eat from it your eyes will be opened, and you will be like God, knowing good and evil."

When the woman saw that the fruit of the tree was good for food and pleasing to the eye, and also desirable for gaining wisdom, she took some and ate it. She also gave some to her husband, who was with her, and he ate it."

(Genesis 3:1-6, NIV)

This scripture shows that from the beginning of time, Satan's main goal is to sway people away from God's goodness. He twists and turns God's words, so that out of them comes confusion and deception. This is why it is so important to know God's Word for yourself, so that you can use it against Satan. When he approached the woman, he started off to make her question God's goodness by saying did God really say you can't eat from ANY tree? Her interpretation of what God said was that they can eat from any of the trees, except the tree in the middle and they couldn't eat from it or touch it, or they would die. God did make it clear to Adam that the tree of knowledge should not be eaten from, but He did not say anything about touching it. So, when Eve also mentioned that they are not to touch it, the serpent was able to use that wiggle room to manipulate the instructions to say that she will not certainly die, but instead, if she ate it, then she will be like God, knowing good and evil. Gaining wisdom enticed her and she chose to go against the instructions of God and followed the serpent's lies to please her flesh. But, where was Adam in all this?

The scripture says that she took a bite and then gave some to Adam who was with her. The scripture does not say that Adam was away from her, nearby from her, or not present with her. It says he was *with her*. If this is the case, then why didn't he intervene on her behalf when she was approached by the serpent, so that he could rebuke the serpent with God's exact command? If he was with her as Scripture says, then it was his responsibility to protect both of them from the serpent's lies. He is supposed to be protecting her, as if he is protecting himself. She is bone and flesh of Adam and he is to love her as his own body. God says in Ephesians for *NO MAN EVER yet hated his own flesh; but nourisheth and cherisheth it.* So, if no man ever, then that means Adam is included and it was his responsibility to make sure that Eve was either nourished properly in God's command for her to rebuke the serpent on her own, or cherished enough that he steps in on her behalf to rebuke the serpent. Eve was not confident enough to be able stand in God's command to be able to withstand the serpent. She interpreted God's command by what she believed and the serpent was able to use the added word to twist and deceive her into the enticement.

The serpent made wisdom seem very appealing, but why would Eve desire wisdom so much that she was willing to disobey the command of God? Eve would not have desired wisdom if it was already given to her in fulfillment. This is why scripture in the New Testament says that the husbands should love their wives like Christ, and wash them through the Word. The Word is our protector and husbands, as leaders, are responsible to lead their wives and children under God's wisdom, so that they are fulfilled and able to use the wisdom against the principalities that will come against them.

"Husbands, love your wives, just as Christ loved the church and gave himself up for her to make her holy, cleansing her by the washing with water through the word, and to present her to himself as a radiant church, without stain or wrinkle or any other blemish, but holy and blameless."

(Ephesians 5:25-27, NIV)

Did Adam give her God's command verbatim or did Eve just not hear him properly? Either way, Adam had a responsibility to remind Eve of what God commanded verbatim, while she was talking to the serpent or had the responsibility to rebuke the serpent by standing firm in God's command himself. Not only did he not protect her against the serpent, but he let her eat the fruit and then ate it too. God told Adam that if he eats from the tree of knowledge, he will die. If Adam loved his own flesh, and indeed cherished it, then he would not have allowed them both to eat the fruit. By eating the fruit himself, knowing that it goes against God's command and he could die, he took that chance anyway, and it signifies that he chose not to hate his own flesh, because Eve was part of his flesh. So, when Eve bit the apple, their flesh *as one* sinned. Adam surely did not hate his own flesh, because **NO MAN EVER** did, but he failed to cherish it or nourish it; otherwise, neither one of them would have fallen for the serpent's tactics. He was present with her, but wasn't there to protect her from the serpent or protect them from eating the fruit. It is not to say that Eve was not responsible for her own actions. She is one-hundred percent responsible for her own desire to eat the fruit and disobeying God's command not to eat it. But, if Adam was with her as the scripture says, then he was responsible for leading Eve away from the serpent and protecting her from the serpent's clever deceit. Adam failed in this and this is why when after they ate the fruit, God called out to Adam.

Okay, now that Adam was the first to fail as a husband, God put a command in place and that is for husbands to love their wives just as Christ loved the church. Well, what does this look like? Let's take a look.

Husbands love your wives, just as Christ loved the church and gave himself up for her

In this verse, it stresses that husbands should love "just as" Christ. That means precisely in the same manner or a degree that is equal to Christ's love for His Church. You are probably thinking that is impossible, the Holy one died for us! You are correct because no one loves greater than He. However, you can love just as He does in such a way, because He is THE example of how He wants you to love your bride-to-be; soon to be wife. First thing to look at is that He gave Himself up for us. There was nothing that stood in the way of Him fulfilling His purpose for our lives. He loved us so much that He willfully gave Himself up to the soldiers who were ready to take Him from Gethsemane, so that He could be brought to King Herod and Pilate. He had the opportunity to boast about who He was, but He gave Himself up to humility. He gave Himself up to the crowd who was not seeking justice, but who wanted to crucify Him. He gave Himself up to the evil soldiers who spat in His face, ridiculed Him, and beat Him until He was unrecognizable and eventually, He gave up Himself to death. He had a choice, but He chose to give up His life for us.

"No one takes it from me, but I lay it down of my own accord. I have authority to lay it down and authority to take it up again. This command I received from my Father."

(John 10:18, NIV)

Why did Jesus give up His life for the Church? Because we were sinners (Romans 5:8) and He wanted to give us the gift of grace and mercy from the law (Romans 3:20-24); Jesus wanted to give the Church life more abundantly (John 10:10); Jesus wanted the Church to live eternally in a better place that is not of this earth (John 3:16); Jesus gave up His life, so that the Church can live and die to their old self (Romans 6:1-23). Okay, now that we understand the reason of giving His life for ours, let's place how He calls husbands to love their wives in the same exact position.

Let's hypothetically ask and put husbands in the same aspect of what Jesus did: Why does [said husband] give up his life for the [said wife]? Because she was a sinner and he wanted to give her the gift of grace and mercy from the law; [Said husband] wanted to give his [said wife] life more abundantly; [Said husband] wanted the [said wife] to live eternally in a better place that is not of this earth; [Said husband] gave up his life, so that the [said wife] can live and die to her old self.

This puts things in a different perspective, doesn't it? It almost makes it seem like Jesus gave up Himself for all of us flawed people, so that we can be saved and in the same sense, husbands should give themselves up for a flawed woman, so that she can be saved. However, this is not quite what this means. It does not mean that wives are less valuable or worthy; both men and woman have equal access to Jesus and everything He died on the cross for us to have. So, it does not mean that husbands should be saving their wives to salvation and it certainly does not mean that husbands are in a better position than wives. What it does mean is that husbands should honor their wives as the weaker vessel.

"Likewise, husbands, live with your wives in an understanding way, showing honor to the woman as the weaker vessel, since they are heirs with you of the grace of life, so that your prayers may not be hindered."

(1 Peter 3:7, NIV)

Understanding that wives are generally spoken of as being physically weaker than husbands is obvious, but not the issue. What this scripture is saying is that wives received the same inheritance of the grace that God has given to husbands, but husbands should understand that they need to treat their wives with more sympathy, gentleness, and endurance, as Jesus does with all of us. Women, by design, are more sensitive, more aware, and more analytical with the affairs of life. Men can easily forget this and become insensitive, and have a lack of understanding how unique women are designed.

To Jesus we, both man and woman, are considered the weaker vessel; we often let our emotions, feelings, and thoughts get in our way, instead of relying on Him to help us with our day to day issues. But, Jesus delights in us when we are humbled enough to let Him be the Lord over us. Jesus is always patient with us, never scorns us, and never leaves us. His grace keeps us and He always has a solution to bring us up. The key here is to understand that Jesus wants to bring us up, because we are the weaker vessel. He wants to make us have strength through Him in everything and wants us to trust in Him. He gave Himself up, so that we can have this kind of relationship with Him. This is how husbands should honor their wives, as being the weaker vessel. A husband should be able to provide an environment where trust is not an issue and where a wife can be built up, knowing that all will be well through their husbands unto Christ.

To make her holy, cleansing her by the washing with water through the Word

Long before Jesus gave His life up for us, He demonstrated something that foreshadowed the gift we were going to receive. He humbly accepted the baptism by John the Baptist.

"I baptize you with water for repentance. But after me comes one who is more powerful than I, whose sandals I am not worthy to carry. He will baptize you with the Holy Spirit and fire. His winnowing fork is in his hand, and he will clear his threshing floor, gathering his wheat into the barn and burning up the chaff with unquenchable fire."

Then Jesus came from Galilee to the Jordan to be baptized by John. But John tried to deter him, saying, "I need to be baptized by you, and do you come to me?"

Jesus replied, "Let it be so now; it is proper for us to do this to fulfill all righteousness." Then John consented.

As soon as Jesus was baptized, he went up out of the water. At that moment heaven was opened, and he saw the Spirit of God descending like a dove and alighting on him. And a voice from heaven said, "This is my Son, whom I love; with him I am well pleased."

(Matthew 3:11-17, NIV)

John the Baptist was a prophet whose mission was to prepare the people for the Messiah. He preached about the coming of Jesus and His perfection. He also preached about the judgments to those who did not repent of their sins and invited them to be baptized by water, so they could be washed of their sins. He was cleansing them by water and his words, symbolizing the death of their sins to be made new. However, since he was only human, he did let the people know that there was someone greater than him that would baptize them with the Holy Spirit, Jesus. The Holy Spirit is the gift that is given to us when we accept Jesus as our Lord and Savior. Without the Holy Spirit, it will be impossible for us to walk towards righteousness and holiness. The Holy Spirit will always, always, always, lead us to do the right thing. Jesus was perfect and never did anything wrong, but by Him getting baptized, He was showing us that He identifies with us and wanted us to know that the washing of the water symbolizes His profound mission to make us holy and cleansed from our sins through Him, because He is the Holy one.

With that being said, how are husbands to make their wives holy and cleanse them with the washing of the Word? It's pretty self-explanatory, but there is more to it than we typically see. As you can see, John the Baptist knew what his purpose was and that was to wash people of their sins through water and the prophesized word. But, he also knew that his mission and purpose was not going to be the way, but that Jesus was going to be the Way. John knew that he was not perfect or sinless than anyone else, but he had an assignment to tell the people about the One who was. Husbands have the responsibility of building their wives up in the Word, but it is not to say that they are holier; it is to recognize that none of us our holy and it is only though Jesus Christ that we can be made holy. Husbands should have the desire to keep himself, his wife, and even his children in Jesus' perfect Holiness. You may be wondering what this looks like; does it look like a husband who should be up on a pulpit preaching to a congregation and baptizing once a month; does it look like a husband dressing his family in all white with bibles in their hands all day long; or does it look like husbands gathering his family three times a day in his living room reading the Bible and talking about it until their ears fall off? No, what it looks like is a husband who simply loves his wife so much that he can't bear to see himself or her outside of God's will. Jesus loved us so much, that He could not bear the thought of us not joining Him in heaven. He could not bear the thought of us staying in our sinful selves. He could not bear the thought of us not being able to have the same access He has to our Heavenly Father. So, He made sure that there was a way for us to be there. Not only be there with Him, but He wanted to be with us here on earth, too. So, we received the Holy Spirit within us that keeps us guided and directed in Him, making us holy and cleansed through Him.

Husbands should love their wives just as much as Jesus does and not bear to want to see their wives drowning in despair, just as Jesus. Husbands should continually remind their wives of who they are in Christ. No matter what may come up against them or their wives as an individual, husbands should love their wives enough to be able to remind them of what Jesus has done for them and what Jesus will do for them. This is cleansing her and encouraging her to renew her mind in Christ and walk in complete awareness of her holiness in Christ. Husbands who love their wives like this, love themselves, as well, and humbly accepts that Jesus is their *everything*.

<u>And to present her to himself as a radiant church, without stain or wrinkle or any other blemish, but holy and blameless</u>

We already know that Jesus is perfect and He lived without sin. He did nothing wrong and He is all good. He has no stain, wrinkle, or blemish. He is the Holy One and blameless in our Heavenly Father's eyes. Here is the good news for us who are in Christ; we are seen the same way in our Heavenly Father's eyes, because of Christ. Jesus, our Savior, Lord, and King of Kings; He is the One who has our back. In our own flesh, we are imperfect people with all kinds of baggage and skeletons in our closet. But, Jesus never presents us this way to our Heavenly Father. He never points out the wrong we have done, the sins we have made, the flaws we have, or the mistakes we have made. When we pray, "In the name of Jesus," all God sees is how we are in Jesus. Isn't that amazing? It's Jesus' blood that covers us in the radiance of beauty. It's through Jesus that we are presented in full holiness and purity. He took on everything that we are, so we can be with Him. In order for Jesus to present us as radiant, He becomes our *everything* to help us along our path. When we are weary, He is there to give us strength; when we are hurt, He is there to heal; when we are down, He is there to encourage; when we make mistakes, He is there to forgive and not condemn; when we feel alone; He is there by our side always; He is our *everything*. So, when it is time to enter the Kingdom of Heaven, He will vouch for us to enter and will do so proudly, because we are His Bride. We are the Bride that God has been sculpting to perfection in Him, so that when it is time to enter the Kingdom of Heaven, we will be blameless, without blemish, stains, or wrinkles. Jesus wants us to be pure perfection and an extension of Him. When Jesus is ready to enter with us into His Kingdom, and God asks why we should enter into Heaven, Jesus will be able to say, because they are perfect like me. What would He look like standing next to His Bride who was not an extension of Himself? Our Father in Heaven would be just like any earthly parent would be, looking at us in question about who we were marrying. If we were still sinners, broken, unrighteous, and worldly while we were standing next to Jesus, we would not at all be an extension of Him. So, because of Jesus we are radiant!

Likewise, husbands should present their wives with radiance and beauty. Husbands should be so supportive in building their wives up in such a way that makes them look and feel as bright as a diamond like Jesus is doing with all of us. God holds you accountable for how you treat your bride and He expects you to present her as an extension of yourself. So, who you are to her will start to show in your bride. Will your bride be a radiant beauty or will she look defeated, beat down, and broken?

Reflection Questions:

Question 1: How will your future bride be an extension of you? Describe what that looks like.

Question 2: If God were to ask Jesus why we should enter into the Kingdom of Heaven with Him, He would be able to say, because it was through Him that we were made whole. If God were to ask you why your bride should marry you, what would you be able to say to Him?

To be the Leader

When God completed the Garden of Eden, He put Adam in it first; the principal or ranking of being a leader. During this time, it was one on one with God. This was his time to understand his Creator and get to know Him, the Father. God had Adam first before Eve, so that the man He created in His own image would dwell in Him, learn from Him, and have a relationship with Him. There is no better leader to learn from, than our Heavenly Father. So, Adam was to be an example as a leader under God's leadership before he was a husband. After Adam and Eve fell short of God's glory and sinned against Him, God called out to the leader.

"Then the man and his wife heard the sound of the LORD God as he was walking in the garden in the cool of the day, and they hid from the LORD God among the trees of the garden. But the LORD God called to the man, "Where are you?"

"He answered, "I heard you in the garden, and I was afraid because I was naked; so I hid."

And he said, "Who told you that you were naked? Have you eaten from the tree that I commanded you not to eat from?"

The man said, "The woman you put here with me—she gave me some fruit from the tree, and I ate it."

Then the LORD God said to the woman, "What is this you have done?"
The woman said, "The serpent deceived me, and I ate."

(Genesis 3:8-13, NIV)

God did not call out to both of them and say, where are you two? He called out to the man, the leader of the household, "Where are you?"After asking Adam if he ate from the tree He commanded him not to eat from, that is when the blame game took place. Adam had an opportunity to confess his lack of being a good example as leader, or protector, for his wife and himself but instead, he put all the blame on her. Eve had the opportunity to confess and say she did not listen to the command that was given to her by her husband, but she blamed the serpent, instead. God did not take heart to their excuses and neither of them asked for forgiveness, so God gave them their consequences. The serpent had a consequence, the woman had a consequence, but God specifically addresses Adam about his disobedience against God's command.

"So the LORD God said to the serpent, "Because you have done this, "Cursed are you above all livestock and all wild animals! You will crawl on your belly and you will eat dust all the days of your life. And I will put enmity between you and the woman, and between your offspring and hers; he will crush your head, and you will strike his heel." To the woman he said, "I will make your pains in childbearing very severe; with painful labor you will give birth to children. Your desire will be for your husband, and he will rule over you."

To Adam he said, "Because you listened to your wife and ate fruit from the tree about which I commanded you, 'You must not eat from it,' "Cursed is the ground because of you; through painful toil you will eat food from it all the days of your life. It will produce thorns and thistles for you, and you will eat the plants of the field. By the sweat of your brow you will eat your food until you return to the ground, since from it you were taken; for dust you are and to dust you will return."

(Genesis 3:14-19, NIV)

The woman was completely responsible for fulfilling her own flesh to eat the fruit. Initially, God blessed them to be fruitful, and increase, and live forever, but because she fulfilled her flesh by eating the forbidden fruit, her consequence was that she was going to bear the fruit of children; her flesh was going to experience severe childbearing pains. What a curse on woman... makes you wonder how pleasant the experience of childbearing would have been had she not eaten the forbidden fruit. But, there is a scripture that completely supports the curse that was put upon her.

"For he that soweth to his flesh shall of the flesh reap corruption; but he that soweth to the Spirit shall of the Spirit reap life everlasting."

(Galatians 6:8, NIV)

In addition to the pains, she was cursed to be ruled over by her husband. Why would God put that on her? God gave Adam instructions not to eat from the tree. Adam gave her God's instruction not to eat from the tree. Since Adam was appointed the leader, then Eve was to follow his leadership. Whether her husband was setting the example as a leader or not, she should have obeyed the command from her husband, because it was God's command. Instead, she fulfilled her own flesh and then led Adam to do the same. Because of yielding to her own desire, God has cursed her with the desire for her husband, but to be ruled over her. We will talk more about this under the wife's role, but this is an example to show that when you are not confident in the wisdom that God has for you, then you can get deceived by the devil. Yes, God did design husbands to be the leader and be a godly example; however, wives, it is still your responsibility to know God's Word for yourself, especially if your husband is not setting the example as a spiritual leader. If you are not careful and not strong in God's Word, then you can be easily confused and set foot into whatever temptation is put before you for lack of confidence. We are all responsible to know God and His wisdom, but God did design the husband as the spiritual leader.

When it came to Adam's consequence, God pointed it out clearly, that he specifically disobeyed His commandment and listened to his wife, instead. God told him exactly what and what not to do, so instead of him listening to his wife, he should have taken his leadership position under God more carefully. He failed as a leader and was cursed to work very hard, in order to provide for his family. Adam had a responsibility as the leader of their territory and that was to lead them in the way God would want them to go. God provided everything and it was all laid out for Adam. All he had to do is care for it, because he was ruler over it. But, because he did not care for the things put before him carefully, he is now cursed with the painful toils of hard work. The painful toils of climbing the corporate ladder, grinding on the chain gangs, and proving the worth of working, so that he can provide and protect. If he would have set the example of his God-given leadership to lead them away from the serpent, then they would not have fallen. If he would have humbled himself and admitted his shortcomings as a leader, the world may have been very different. Instead of holding himself accountable for his own disobedience, he looked for someone else to blame.

Because of Adam's fall, God already knew what command had to take place today for husbands, which we already discussed earlier, but let's see why He commanded this based on Adam's failure.

"Husbands, love your wives, just as Christ loved the church and gave himself up for her to make her holy, cleansing her by the washing with water through the word, and to present her to himself as a radiant church, without stain or wrinkle or any other blemish, but holy and blameless."

(Ephesians 5:25-27, NIV)

When God was looking for Adam to explain his own actions for eating the fruit that God commanded him not to eat from, he voluntarily and quickly blamed Eve for his shortcoming. If you read scripture very carefully, at no point did God directly command Eve not to eat from the tree; He directly commanded Adam not to eat from it. Under his leadership, he was responsible to give Eve the instructions, which he obviously did. However, when the serpent manifested its plans, Adam was not there to protect her, he was not there to guide her, he disobeyed God for her, and then he ate the fruit to die with her. In the above scripture, God makes it very clear that husbands are to love their wives like Christ loves the Church. To do this, husbands would need to love their wives in the opposite way that Adam did. He is to love her in such a way that makes her holy and a reflection, or extension, of himself as unto Christ as the radiant Church. Jesus gave us the teachings of the Word and set Himself as an example of the Word. Jesus loved us despite our flaws, our temperaments, and our sins. He laid down His life willingly, so that we were forgiven and made to be seen as righteous in our Father's eyes. Our Father sees no wrong in us, because of Jesus. He sees no blemish, no stain, and no wrinkle. We are made holy and are represented as holy through Christ. In Adam's case, he did not love his wife in this way. He did not wash her in the Word; instead, he let her get deceived by the serpent's word. He pointed out her wrongdoing and blamed her for his own disobedience. He was not representing himself in the likeness of God that created him nor was he presenting Eve as a radiant extension of himself.

There is one thing which stood out that Adam did for his wife and that was to lay down his life by eating the fruit with her. Why did he do this? Why did he eat the fruit even though he knew he would die? Perhaps he may have had good intentions, because she was flesh of his flesh and he did not want her to suffer the consequences alone. Despite, he still had a choice; either to obey God to have the chance to live forever, or disobey God and die. He chose to disobey God and lay down his life for his wife and with her to live in sin. His emotions got in the way of his obedience to God.

"Then the eyes of both of them were opened, and they realized they were naked; so they sewed fig leaves together and made coverings for themselves."

(Genesis 3:7, NIV)

Consuming the forbidden fruit caused their eyes to be opened to sin, shame, and guilt. They put off their desires to obey God and decided to desire their own things. They died from living eternally and they also died to themselves from purity. Eve desired wisdom and Adam laid down his life for his desire of his wife; all done out of disobedience to God.

Let's recap, husbands were designed to provide, protect, and be the leader of their household; not just monetarily, but emotionally and more importantly under God's instruction for life in all those areas. Husbands, God gave you a huge responsibility, because you have the attributes of God to be able to fulfill this role. The only reason why you would not be able to fulfill this role is if you choose not to. The story of Adam testifies what happens when you choose not to fulfill the role that God has given you under His instruction. I want to make it very clear that Adam was not responsible for Eve's action; he was responsible for protecting and being a leading example, in order to lead her away from the serpent for a better life. In today's world, there are many serpents lingering around to put temptation in your household, especially you. It is your leadership that God relies on to build a family that represents Christ. You are the *Adam* that the serpent wants so that you have no chance of leading your family under God's design and the serpent will use anyone he can to get to you, so that he can destroy your God-given leadership, causing families to be corrupt. He will use people, your job, finances, circumstances, and more.

The serpents' ultimate goal is to destroy the family that God designed, so that His glory is diminished. The only way you can combat that is through God's Word and nourishing your family with God's Word. In your own strength, you will not be able to keep your family upright and in God's will. God does not desire you to conquer the world in your own strength. He wants you to trust Him and rely solely upon Him. If you seek wholeheartedly for God's guidance, provision, and desire for your family, then you will be not perfect, but a great leader, provider, and protector. The family that God gave you is His gift to you, wouldn't you want to show God your gratitude by caring for them in the way that He instructs you to? Don't be the Adam who did not stand strong in his obedience to God the moment the serpent came into the picture. Be on guard at all times. I'll leave you with one more scripture on your role as the leader of your family and you can interpret what that means to you.

"Whoever brings ruin on their family will inherit only wind, and the fool will be servant to the wise."

(Proverbs 11:29, NIV)

Wife's role

"For man did not come from woman, but woman from man; neither was man created for woman, but woman for man."

(1 Corinthians 11:8-9, NIV)

A friend of mine and I were talking one day and the question came up, why does it seem like women have to endure so much from their husbands? In her observation, she believes that more women go through so much with their husbands than vise versa. Based on the many marriages that I've observed, including my past marriage, it does seem to appear that way. However, I had to really think about that, do wives really have to endure so much more than husbands? To wives, it may seem like we married someone who is mentally behind in years, has no listening or communicating skills, shuts down every time we open our mouths, does not like to share in any way; especially financially, shows no affection, no emotion, insensitive, workaholics, and the list can go on. In addition, with the more difficult challenges, husbands seem to easily fall into sexual affairs, become addicts of some sort, can be mentally or physically abusive, secretive, manipulative, controlling, etc. These just seem to be the things that many wives can relate to with other wives. It is not to say that all husbands are like this, but it does seem like wives have to deal with so much in their marriages, because of these types of challenges in their husbands. But, if you ask husbands why they go through more than wives, they will tell you that woman think they are always right, they think men are mind-readers, their expectations are too high, they are not sexual enough, they are too emotional, they compare them to other men, undermine their leadership, put others or other things before him, dishonoring or disrespectful, nagging, too sensitive, and their list can also go on. The more difficult challenges can include the same as what husbands do, but are not as highly likely. So, why do wives seem to go through more than husbands in their marriages? The answer is this; husbands go though more than you think. In addition to the high pressures of being the provider, the protector, and the leader of their homes, they have the pressures on their jobs and the spiritual warfare that comes up against them in life in general is unlike any-thing that most women go through. The fact is, wives and husbands endure much, but just differently. Unless we can magically switch places, then we will never understand each other's endurances and will always feel like the other person has it easier. God has roles for wives, too, but He designed them so differently; so much more like Him to be a unique compliment to their husbands. That compliment is called, *the helper*.

"The LORD God said, "It is not good for the man to be alone. I will make a helper suitable for him."

(Genesis 2:18, NIV)

The helper

When God created the heavens and the earth in His own timing, He admired each of His completed missions by saying that it was *good*. When He created mankind in His own image, he said it was good, but not until after He finished creating both man and woman. When He created Adam first, He said that it was not good for man to be alone. Adam was not alone, He had a relationship with God that was good, but God saw that it was not good for man to be alone on earth, so He created a woman to be his suitable *helper*. Creating both man and woman completed all that He had in mind to make and when it was completed, He said it was VERY good.

"God saw all that he had made, and it was very good. And there was evening, and there was morning—the sixth day."

(Genesis 1:22, NIV)

So, what does this mean? It means that without woman, a man alone is not good. God created woman to make man complete; to make the unity of man and woman complete, the union of oneness complete, the trinity of man and woman created in the image of God complete. A woman is a vital part of complete wholeness. God created you to be the suitable helper for your *Adam*. Your Adam is flawed, but so are you. The difference is God gave you a different kind of strength and a way to love. I wanted to elaborate why God specifically called the woman a suitable helper for man.

The word "helper" is used to describe one other important role. Jesus tells us that it is a gift that can only be obtained as a believer and how its purpose is to be a Helper to us. That role is what we have come to know as, the *Holy Spirit*.

"On one occasion, while he was eating with them, he gave them this command: "Do not leave Jerusalem, but wait for the gift my Father promised, which you have heard me speak about. For John baptized with water, but in a few days you will be baptized with the Holy Spirit."

(Acts 1:4-5, NIV)

"But the Helper, the Holy Spirit, whom the Father will send in My name, He will teach you all things, and bring to your remembrance all things that I said to you."

(John 14:26, NIV)

65

It is pretty amazing to know that as a woman, you are called a *helper* just as the Holy Spirit is called, a *Helper*. It is not to say that you completely function like the Helper, but you have similar attributes as the Helper that were given to you to bring purpose to the union. You are a gift and women are more sensitive to hear the Spirit, because of their sensitive attribute of what we call *intuition*. Not only is the Spirit called the Helper, but it is described as good.

"You gave your good Spirit to instruct them. You did not withhold your manna from their mouths, and you gave them water for their thirst."

(Nehemiah 9:20, NIV)

How fitting. God did not call man good, until the woman was united to him. So, now that you know that you have an important role as a helper, what is your divine purpose to being your soon-to-be husband's suitable helper? Let's take a look at some of the attributes of what the Helper, the Holy Spirit, is and how you are called to be a similar helper.

The Holy Spirit as Wisdom

Have you ever wondered why Adam never wanted to go to the tree of knowledge to find out about good and evil? He was there before Eve and he certainly had the opportunity. God gave him direct orders not to eat from the tree and he initially obeyed neither was he tempted by the serpent at anytime. The serpent knew that it could not tempt Adam, so in craftiness, he laid out a plan. That plan was to go through Eve, in order to get to Adam. When the serpent tempted Eve, she saw that the fruit from the tree was good for food and was pleasing to the eye. There were plenty of trees in the garden for good food and pleasing, but what made this one more desirable to her was something called, *wisdom*. She was willing to go against her husband's leadership to gain her own wisdom. She certainly went about gaining the wisdom in the wrong way to receive it, but the fact of the matter is, she desired to receive it and then wanted her husband to receive the wisdom, too.

*"That the Father of glory, may give to you the **Spirit of wisdom** and revelation in the knowledge of Him."*

(Ephesians 1:17, KJV, emphasis)

I love the book of Proverbs because it addresses wisdom as being feminine. Part of Proverbs shows a comparison between wisdom and folly. It addresses both as females; wisdom builds up and folly tears down. Although, Proverbs is to be read more like a book of poetry, it still gives off a kind of sense that wisdom signifies female attributes of God and what He uses in woman to be the helper for husbands. Here are some of the verses from Proverbs starting at Proverbs 3 where the title is *Wisdom Bestows in Well-Being*, which means wisdom that is applied for a good state of satisfied condition of existence (remember this).

"Blessed are those who find wisdom, those who gain understanding, for she is more profitable than silver and yields better returns than gold. She is more precious than rubies; nothing you desire can compare with her. Long life is in her right hand; in her left hand are riches and honor. Her ways are pleasant ways, and all her paths are peace. She is a tree of life to those who take hold of her; those who hold her fast will be blessed."

(Proverbs 3:13-18, NIV)

"Do not forsake wisdom, and she will protect you; love her, and she will watch over you. The beginning of wisdom is this: Get wisdom. Though it cost all you have, get understanding. Cherish her, and she will exalt you; embrace her, and she will honor you. She will give you a garland to grace your head and present you with a glorious crown."

(Proverbs 4:6-9, NIV)

In these scriptures, it starts by pointing out how blessed those are who find wisdom. Wisdom is knowledge and instruction for how to live in righteousness. So, those who receive it will be blessed. Wisdom is for our own protection and nothing compares to having wisdom, because it is more than silver and gold. The book of Proverbs makes it clear that the Spirit of Wisdom's sole purpose and desire is to help, not hinder.

This can be said in the same way of wives who are the husbands' helper. When I use the term *wisdom* for wives, it is not to say that she is Godly wisdom, but she is signified as wisdom; which means that it is the virtue to think and act using insight, knowledge, common sense, good judgment, experience, and understanding. The first instance where wives can be likened to the Holy Spirit of Wisdom is in the book of Proverbs. It says blessed are those who find wisdom. The book also says that about finding a wife.

"He who finds a wife finds a good thing, And obtains favor from the LORD."

(Proverbs 18:22, NIV)

"A wife of noble character who can find? She is worth far more than rubies. Her husband has full confidence in her and lacks nothing of value. She brings him good, not harm, all the days of her life "

(Proverbs 1:10-12, NIV)

Soon-to-be wives, first thing you should know is you are a good find for your soon-to-be husband, and it is because of you that he obtains favor from the Lord. That's a big deal! Do you know why he obtains favor from the Lord when he finds you? He finds favor, because you are the *wisdom* that will be a part of helping him to his understanding of whom he is and who he will become. Yes, you will be a part of that. But, hold on, before you go boast to tell him how important you are to this marriage, you must understand what God says about wisdom, in order to fulfill your role as wisdom to help him.

"But the wisdom that comes from heaven is first of all pure; then peace-loving, considerate, submissive, full of mercy and good fruit, impartial and sincere."

(James 3:17, NIV)

This scripture could not have described wisdom any better. As a wife, the next paragraphs will focus on how the wisdom in you manifests towards your husband.

Wisdom is Pure

If you read the book of Proverbs, you will notice how scripture compares wisdom to folly. Between the two, the first thing to recognize is that wisdom's motives are pure and folly's motives are impure.

"Wisdom has built her house; she has set up its seven pillars. She has prepared her meat and mixed her wine; she has also set her table. She has sent out her servants, and she calls from the highest point of the city, "Let all who are simple come to my house!"To those who have no sense she says, "Come, eat my food and drink the wine I have mixed. Leave your simple ways and you will live; walk in the way of insight."Whoever corrects a mocker invites insults; whoever rebukes the wicked incurs abuse.

Do not rebuke mockers or they will hate you; rebuke the wise and they will love you. Instruct the wise and they will be wiser still; teach the righteous and they will add to their learning. The fear of the LORD is the beginning of wisdom, and knowledge of the Holy One is understanding. For through wisdom your days will be many, and years will be added to your life. If you are wise, your wisdom will reward you; if you are a mocker, you alone will suffer.

Folly is an unruly woman; she is simple and knows nothing. She sits at the door of her house, on a seat at the highest point of the city, calling out to those who pass by, who go straight on their way, "Let all who are simple come to my house!" To those who have no sense she says, "Stolen water is sweet; food eaten in secret is delicious!"

But little do they know that the dead are there, that her guests are deep in the realm of the dead."

(Proverbs 9:1-18, NIV)

Wisdom promises the rewards of long life, insight, happiness, contentment, and fulfillment. You can read this in detail on your own in Proverbs 8. Folly promises death, deceit, and sin. In the above scripture, they both call out to those who are simple; who have no sense, and they both invite them, so they can be fed. However, one of them has pure intentions and the other does not. As a wife when you want to speak something to your husband, ask yourself what are your intentions? Are they pure or are your intents to manipulate, nag, or provoke? Wisdom and Folly both had something to say, but which one of them who is calling out, is being heard? If you are the wife of wisdom, then you will be heard through the next attribute of wisdom which is *peace-loving.*

Wisdom is peace-loving and considerate

Wives you do have something to say to offer your husbands, but how are you calling out to him to receive it? Are you the woman who calls out to life or the woman who calls out to death? Where are you getting your wisdom from? Is it directly from God or is it from the serpent that deceived you to obtain it? Are you the one who is speaking out of love or are you the one speaking out of terror?

*"For, 'Whoever would love life and see good days must keep his tongue from evil and his lips from deceitful speech. He must turn from evil and do good; he must seek **peace** and pursue it. For the eyes of the Lord are on the righteous and his ears are attentive to their prayer, but the face of the Lord is against those who do evil."*

(1 Peter 3:10-12, NIV, emphasis)

Your words can help or hurt your spouse. Your words can encourage your spouse or repress your spouse. Your words can bring loving peace or can cause nagging uproars. Your words can transform your spouse or make them stagnate. Yes, your words are important to your spouse and can influence him to a **good state of satisfied condition of existence.**

To be *peace-loving* means not to cause strife, bitter envy, sorrow, or anger. To be considerate means to be aware of other's feelings and watch how you communicate to them. God gave you the ability to help bring your husband to a better state of his existence, but by being very careful of how you speak. You know the worldly saying; *behind every good man is a good wife.* This is also true biblically. There are some great wives in the Bible that were united to their husbands to be their helpers. Some of the wives in the Bible had their flaws, but each distinctly had purpose to influence their husbands to their destiny by displaying *peace-loving* and *considerate wisdom.*

Wisdom is submissive

Godly wisdom focuses on God and God alone. So, when Scripture says that wisdom is submissive, then it means when we hear God's wisdom, we are submitting to who He is and who He is alone. We submit to His wisdom, because we know what is true and what is good. We know that God will never give us instruction that will destroy us or leave us in desolate adversity. He will never command something for us to do if there was not purpose behind it. When we instruct our kids to do their homework, study, and get good grades, they may not really want to do it or even like to do it. But, we are telling them because we know the end result of getting good grades; good grades gets you to graduation; gets you scholarships; gets you into college; gets you a college degree; can land you a good career; can give you financial security. We see the purpose of what can happen when they submit to our instruction that leads to the end result of financial security. God gave us His wisdom for purpose. He knows the end result of everything that pertains to our lives, which is why when we submit to His wisdom, we are reaping the benefits of His end results for our lives. With this being concrete in understanding, then when God says wives submit to your husbands, we should believe the end result is for God's purpose.

"Wives, submit yourselves to your own husbands as you do to the Lord. For the husband is the head of the wife as Christ is the head of the church, his body, of which he is the Savior. Now as the church submits to Christ, so also wives should submit to their husbands in everything."

(Ephesians 5:22-24, NIV)

When you submit to God, you are putting all your trust in Him, because you know that His plans for you are good. He does not promise you that trusting in Him means you will have a blissful time during the process of getting to His purposely filled plans for you, but He does promise you that His plans for you are good. Likewise, He says to submit yourself to your husband in the same way that you submit to Him. He is not going to promise you that if you submit to your husbands, as you do Him, that it will be all bliss, but if you submit to His wisdom, He promises you that His plan for you doing so will be good. It's easy when you know that your husband is wholeheartedly seeking God's wisdom for your unity and everything that is attached to your unity. But, this can be so hard for many wives to submit to their husbands, because of the fear of what could happen if they submit to the leadership of someone who isn't seeking wisdom from God. So, while you are still in the stages of being engaged, are you willing to be with someone who is not seeking Godly wisdom? If you are, then it is your free will to do so, but please keep this in mind that there are some instances where you may be led by someone who is leading you down the wrong path. There were many leaders of Israel that God clearly said were evil in His eyes, because they led His people down the wrong path. If you choose to marry someone who does not seek Godly wisdom, then you are subjecting yourself to follow this instruction of submitting yourself to someone, and it could be a long battle. However, even if you choose to marry someone who does not seek Godly wisdom, then you will just have to trust God that His instruction will eventually work out for your good in His own way and His own time.

Good news is that He commands you to submit to your husband, but as you do Him. He does not just say, submit to your husbands. He knows that if we were to just submit to our husbands without Him, then yes, we are looking for a very uncertain road. But, instead, He says as you do Him. So, as long as you are in full submission to God, then you are in His good perfect will for everything in your life, including your marriage. Even if your husband is not seeking Godly wisdom, God is there for you and He honors your submission to His Word. Now, this does not mean that you should submit to your husband when evil doings are present. What is wrong is wrong and you are not asked to submit to such. When you submit to God, you are submitting to nothing but good, because He is all good. There is nothing bad about Him, but the same cannot be said for us, but particularly for your husband in this chapter. Your husband may want to do things not in accordance to God's teaching, but if he does, then you are required to speak out wisdom in hopes that the truth will dwell in him. There may be some things that will happen out of his own accountability as consequences for your husband not seeking Godly wisdom, but because of your submission to God first, His grace will step in and each time that it does, it will reveal things to your husband that can win him over to want to seek God more. It is still his choice, but it is what you can hope that God can change in his heart. A better way to look at it is that there is more to who your mate is than what you see. God has purpose and good plans for him too, and by you being the submissive wife to your husband as unto God, you are put in a position as "the helper" to bring him more and more into God's plan for his life. However, this is why it is so important to know who you are selecting as a lifetime partner for a husband. You want to make sure that you choose a husband who does submit to the Lord, because that is God's best for you.

"And if a woman has a husband who is not a believer and he is willing to live with her, she must not divorce him. For the unbelieving husband has been sanctified through his wife, and the unbelieving wife has been sanctified through her believing husband."

(1 Corinthians 7:13-14, NIV)

You as "the helper" who submits to God's wisdom are a part of God's plan for your husband, so submission to your husband is all part of trusting Him and knowing that He has good purpose. He is not instructing you to submit to your husband unto Him to harm you; He is instructing you to submit to your husband, because He has the end result and plans not only for you, but your husband, as well. You were called to be your future husband's equal partner through *submission*.

Wisdom is full of mercy and good fruit

"Be merciful, just as your Father is merciful."

(Luke 6:36, NIV)

Over the years, many of us viewed God as this Father who was ready to punish and scorn us the minute we did something against Him. It was preached in churches, taught in our homes, and passed on to generations. Many of us grew up in fear of God. However, God is so far from that image and we are coming into the age of truth where we can now see God as one of compassion, slow to anger, patient, comforting, and gracious. All done out of His mercy. Let's face it, we have all done some horrible and sinful things in our lives that we are not proud of and we all deserve judgment and condemnation. We have all fallen short of God's glory and unfortunately, we will, at some point, fall more than once of His glory. However, because of God's love and His mercy, we have been redeemed from our punishment unjustly, but justly in Jesus. I don't know about you, but I am extremely glad that He is a God of compassion and that He continues to be merciful for a person like me, who can be quite stubborn. If there is anything you are getting from this, know that God is always, always good and there is nothing bad about Him. So, get the bad image you may have about Him, and lock it somewhere far away.

We can't be as merciful as God, it is very hard to because we do have some bad attributes in us that will prevent us from wanting to do what is good. It's our flesh and we most certainly can't help that. But, He does instruct us to be merciful, just as He is. As... meaning, to the same degree or measure. Wow, who can do this? Absolutely...not one...of any... of us... can in our own strength. So, why would God instruct us to do something that only He can do, because of who He

74

is? Once again, it is not a matter of what we can do or even want to do; it is a matter of submitting to His wisdom. So, wives, when husbands do some things to you that are hurtful, deceitful, or even downright despicable, the first flesh's reaction wants more than anything to throw in the towel and just step out of the virtuous wife's nature to become the vindictive green witch from the Wizard of Oz. But, you know what God says, no baby girl... BE MERCIFUL. Husbands are going to fail you, just like you are going to fail your husbands in some way or another, but God gave you an endurance that does not compare to your husband's endurance. Your husband's endurance is more physical and mental, but your endurance is more emotional and merciful. Since you are "the helper," what better teacher do you have than "The Helper" where you can have mercy that can only come through the fruits of the Holy Spirit?

"But the fruit of the Spirit is love, joy, peace, forbearance, kindness, goodness, faithfulness, gentleness and self-control. Against such things there is no law."

(Galatians 5:22-23, NIV)

This is the good fruit in which the wisdom of mercy feeds. You will have to rely on the fruits of the Spirit, in order to have mercy towards your husband. You cannot do it on your own. The Holy Spirit can fill you up with His fruit, so that it pours out into your husband. Your husband may not deserve anything if he has wronged you, but God says, BE MERCIFUL and be as merciful as Him to the same degree. The Holy Spirit is powerful and successful to accomplish being merciful as He instructs you to be. You may not have the gift of being merciful, but you, "the helper," have "The Helper" to show you the example.

Wisdom is impartial and sincere

"For there is no partiality with God."

(Romans 2:11, ESV)

God makes it very clear that He does not show partiality to anyone. He does not treat people differently because of their status, the way they look, the way they act, if they are a Jew or Gentile, or if they are a Christian or a Muslim. He can use whoever He wants to accomplish His purpose of salvation. He sees us all the same, which is His children and He does not favor one over the other. You may be thinking, well why are some people more blessed than others? Yes, God does bless people in different ways, but you can't judge that God loves and shows favoritism over others. You don't know what they had to experience to receive the works of God for their blessings. Their blessings are for them and God blessed them for His sole purpose to show His existence. But, He is not putting anyone on a higher pedestal than the other. We all have our blessings in some form or another and we should be glad that God does not show partiality based on who we are, because then we would all get what we deserve, which would be death, instead of life.

"But if you show partiality, you are committing sin and are convicted by the law as transgressors."

(James 2:9, ESV)

Sometimes, we can all get in a state where we are comparing our spouse to another spouse or we treat other people better than we treat our own spouse. We can get into this idea that our spouse does not deserve to be treated with the fruit of the Spirit, because of what they have done to hurt us, or the way they act, or who they are in general. Because women are more emotional, wives tend to do this more than they realize it and if they do realize it, they feel justified to be able to do so. Let me stress this very clearly, husbands do not take it very well when you compare him to other men. That is the same vice versa, but men are not as verbal and bold-faced about comparing as women. Women can get very crafty in their worldly wisdom and believe that comparing will magically turn a light bulb on in their spouses head to become a better husband. They will use their fathers, brothers, neighbors, T.V. celebrities, pastors, etc., to set an example of what a husband should be. For example, something as little as saying, "My father took out the trash every night and my mother never had to do that chore" can be interpreted as, "You are so lazy, why can't you do the same you no good man?" Or when the father does come around, they go all out of the way to make them comfortable and forget that the husband is even there. Yet, to them, it is justified, because the husband is not like the father and the father deserves to be treated better, because of what kind of husband he was. While the father may have appeared to be a good husband, you may have no idea what went on in your parent's relationship. So, it would not be fair to judge your husband against your father. You also cannot compare, because your husband is not the same as someone else. He has different temperaments, different backgrounds, different philosophies, and different views. But, because of the goal of one flesh, those are the very things that God is using to work his blessings in your marriage. Good or bad attributes of your husband, God knows what to use for His purpose for you, your husband, your children, and everyone else around you.

"The goal of this command is love, which comes from a pure heart and a good conscience and a sincere faith. [6] Some have departed from these and have turned to meaningless talk. [7] They want to be teachers of the law, but they do not know what they are talking about or what they so confidently affirm."

(1 Timothy 1:5-7, NIV)

From the beginning of time, starting with Eve, wives have had a strong desire for wisdom and not only have it, but share it, starting with sharing it with Adam. However, we must understand there is worldly wisdom and Godly wisdom. Worldly wisdom is not confidently affirmed. When Adam gave Eve God's commandment not to eat from the tree, she received the commandant secondhand, not directly from God. Since, she did not receive it verbatim, she was not confident when trying to state it herself, leaving it open for the serpent to use it to his advantage.

In 1 Timothy 1:5-7, he describes people who are speaking in false doctrines and are not giving sincere wisdom from God, which robs God short of the glory He deserves. People want to be teachers of the law, but when they speak, they are not confident. As a helper, you should be able to speak to your spouse so that they understand you and what message you are trying to send them. However, make sure that your yes is *yes* and your no is *no*; meaning, speak sincerely enough, so that they do not have to read between the lines. Because of logical thinking, most men are black and white, so speaking in meaningless talk will only cause speculation. Before speaking, ask God to show you how to speak in a loving and sincere manner, so that you do not come across as not having enough confidence in what you are saying. Make sure it is wisdom that aligns with the teachings of God.

The Holy Spirit Intercedes with Prayer

"But if we hope for what we do not see, we wait for it with patience. Likewise the Spirit helps us in our weakness. For we do not know what to pray for as we ought, but the Spirit himself intercedes for us with groanings too deep for words. And he who searches hearts knows what is the mind of the Spirit, because the Spirit intercedes for the saints according to the will of God."

(Romans 8:25-26, ESV)

The Holy Spirit is such a special gift, because He knows what to pray for even when we do not always know what to pray for ourselves. When we get the overwhelming feelings of sorrow, condemnation, doubt, fear, frustration, anger, sadness, and even good feelings of joy and love, we sometimes don't know how to contain them or what to do with them. Have you ever been in a circumstance where it just seems unbearable, had thoughts that control you, or been in a position where you just don't know how to handle the situation? When we are in those times of being overwhelmed, that is when we have the privilege to rely on the Holy Spirit to intercede on our behalf and lift prayers up to our Father. We do not always know what to pray for, but because God knows our hearts and has His perfect will for our lives, the Spirit knows exactly when to ignite the power of prayer and what to pray for. The Holy Spirit then reveals things to you to act upon. There is a book I read entitled, *Holy Spirit, The Promise Left for the Believer*, by Deborah G. Hunter. This book gives great insight on how the Holy Spirit operates as a person. She points out something that is relevant to what I am going to explain as the role of the wife; she says "The Holy Spirit opens the eyes and ears of our spirit and downloads heavenly insight and revelation."

God desires the husband to be the spiritual leader of the household and to be able to pray for his family and more intimately, with his wife. There are many husbands who are those praying warriors for their family, but there are also some that are not. But, as a wife, you can be a blessing to your husband and intercede on his behalf. Since "The Helper" intercedes in prayer according to God's will, you as "the helper" can intercede according to God's will for your husband, too. The Holy Spirit will open the eyes and ears of your spirit and download heavenly insight and revelation. Husband's have more trials and tribulations than you may think. You may not always know the struggles that he has to face on his job, or the struggles he has within himself, but you will know that prayer is needed. The Holy Spirit will reveal things to you that your husband will not even know that he needs for himself. There will be times that you will not always know his struggles and may not agree with how he is reacting to them; you may even start judging him as an ungodly man. You have a choice to both sit there and judge your husband for something you don't understand or a choice to be that helper to pray for him, so that he will become what God has called him to be. As the helper, God expects you to pray for your husband in ways that only you can pray, because you are his life-long partner. What will be revealed to you will not only benefit your husband, but will benefit you as a couple.

There are obvious things that you should pray toward your husband, like obedience to God's will and plan for his life, that wisdom is revealed to him and dwells in his heart, that he is encompassed with God's love to experience God's Heavenly Fatherhood like no other father on earth, that he loves you like Christ loves the Church and raises the children under the instruction of Jesus, and to be a good provider. But, when there are other things that are bigger than you can imagine, like spiritual warfare, then that is when you start praying for the armor of God to guard his heart. You will be on your knees time after time for this husband of yours, but please don't get weary of doing so, or you will miss out on receiving the blessings that were sown out of praying labor. Just like God gave husbands huge responsibility to care for you, He is also giving you a very important responsibility to care for your husband. You, "the helper," are truly an amazing gift to your husband and you are the praying warrior and conqueror that can bring him to his highest place of existence simply by your prayers.

The Holy Spirit Encourages

"And I will ask the Father, and he will give you another advocate to help you and be with you forever—the Spirit of truth. The world cannot accept him, because it neither sees him nor knows him. But you know him, for he lives with you and will be in you."

(John 14:16-17, NIV)

Once we accept Jesus Christ as our Lord and Savior, we receive the Holy Spirit as a gift. The Holy Spirit is an amazing gift, because He dwells in us and lives with us forever. The Holy Spirit is our Advocate, someone who supports us, comforts us, and encourages us. The Holy Spirit works within us to be righteous and will always encourages us. Since the Spirit is truth, then anything that is put in your mind that is a lie is from the Devil. The Spirit will always, always, always be in you to encourage and lead you in the right direction. Without our Advocate, we will be lost, confused, lack confidence, and in torment, all from the Devil. So, we should seek daily and consistently for our encouraging Holy Spirit to keep us from entering into a discouraging place.

"Who can find a virtuous woman? for her price is far above rubies. The heart of her husband doth safely trust in her, so that he shall have no need of spoil. She will do him good and not evil all the days of her life."

(Proverbs 31: 10-12, KJV)

Here is the best time to answer the question of why it seems like woman have to go through so much more with their husbands than vice versa. The answer is simple, because you are more like *The Helper*; The Holy Spirits' attribute of God who is naturally loving, wise, faithful, patient, safe, and incomparable to anything else, even rubies. Men go through so much as well, but just differently. But, because women have more of The Helper attributes, men are not going to battle the same principalities towards their wives, as wives do with their husbands. Their principalities are more against the world that they have to face daily to be the provider, protector, and spiritual leader. God commands them to sacrifice their lives for their wives like Christ does. That is not an easy job! So, as wives, you should be the encourager that your husband needs to put on the armor against his sacrifices for you. Always be the encourager and bring good to his life, even when you do not feel like you should. Encouraging can do a whole lot more than no encouragement at all. You have the attributes to be *Holy-Sprit like*, just like your husband should be *Christ-like*.

Reflection Questions:

Question 1: What are your views for being considered your mate's helper?

Question 2: Is your mate someone that you feel you can submit to as unto the Lord? Why or Why not?

Chapter 3

Against Being Joined Together

"Haven't you read," he replied, "that at the beginning the Creator 'made them male and female,' and said, 'For this reason a man will leave his father and mother and be united to his wife, and the two will become one flesh'? So they are no longer two, but one flesh. Therefore what God has joined together, let no one separate."

(Matthew 19:4-6, NIV)

*A*fter God created the heavens and the earth, He created Adam. Adam was His first human creation and He had a one on one relationship with Him. He talked with him, instructed him, and directed him, but most importantly He created him in the likeness of Him. Adam was a tiny extension of who God is; which means that Adam was whole. He was whole because of several factors. The first and foremost reason why he was whole was because he had a very intimate relationship with God. The second reason he was whole, was after God created the Garden of Eden, Adam was put on the earth first. First; the principal or ranking of being a leader. So, Adam started off as being a leader. The third reason of his wholeness was, God gave Adam an assignment to work and take care of what was created. Adam was able to cultivate, nurture, and tend to everything that was in the Garden of Eden. There was nothing more that God had to do for Adam because he was made in His likeness and he was given everything to make him whole as a man. However, even though Adam as a man was whole, God made one thing clear and that is it was not good for a man to be alone. What man was not good to be alone? The man that was already whole because of his likeness of who he was and who he represented, which was God. So, when it was time to join Eve to Adam, Eve was brought to a man who was whole. God could have joined Eve to a man who was confused, who was immature, who was uncertain, who was lazy, who was anything but whole in God. But, when God was ready to join the one man and the one woman together, He did not join them until His work with Adam was complete. Once His work was complete in Adam, He then created woman by taking a rib from Adam. Eve was complete after she was made from a man who was whole so that God could join them together to become one flesh; one flesh in the likeness of Him.

Do you see how God's timing was perfect in this? His best timing to join them was when Adam was whole. He joined two people and considered it His best work. When we start dating and looking for our potential lifelong spouse, it can be easy to overlook what God would want joined together. People can argue that when scripture says what God has joined together it means that any couple who gets married, then God joined them together. But, really think about this statement. Would God join a woman to someone who is physically abusive? Would God join a woman to a man who has no desire to work? Would God join a woman to a substance abuser? Would God join light and dark together, or evil and good together? The answer is simply, *no*. If a woman chooses to join herself with a man who is not whole in Christ, then it was simply her own choice. By now, you are probably wondering why I am using examples of what type of man God would not join a woman to and not vice versa.

Again, I stress the importance of when God joined the man and woman together. He did not join them until Adam was whole. He also stresses that a man will leave his mother and father and unite to his wife, not vice versa. Eve was not complete until she was formed by Adam. But, at the same time, it was not good for a whole man to be alone, so Eve was also a completion to man, but in an entirely different way. But, for now, yes I am stressing the importance of when God joined man and woman together, it was after He made Adam a whole man. When I say this, it reminds me of a comment someone made about how God does sometimes put together a couple who are unequally yoked, so that He can use one person to help bring another person to Christ. The example they used was the story of Hosea and Gomer.

"This was the LORD's first message to Hosea. The LORD said, "Go, marry a prostitute who has had children as a result of her prostitution. Do this because the people in this country have acted like prostitutes—they have been unfaithful to the LORD."

(Hosea 2, ERV)

Hosea was a Prophet, a man who was whole and obedient to God, so obedient that when he was asked to go and marry a prostitute, he humbly took the command and sought after Gomer who continued to commit unfaithful acts towards her husband as a prostitute. You are probably thinking, well, this obviously goes against the point early in question on whether or not God would join a woman with an abuser, etc., or in this case, join someone with a prostitute. This point still holds true because again, I stress that Hosea was a whole man who sought after God's heart. Because Hosea was a man who sought after God's heart, God could trust him to do His will and purpose for the marriage He wanted to join together. In addition to the joining of this type of marriage, the focus is not the fact that Hosea, a whole man, married a flawed woman, but to show the relationship that God had with the Israelites. Take a look at why God told Hosea to marry Gomer.

"Then the Lord said to me again, Gomer has many lovers, but you must continue loving her. Do this because it is an example of the Lord's love for Israel. He continues to love them, but they continue to turn to their gods, and they love to eat those raisin cakes."

(Hosea 3:1, ERV)

He clearly told Hosea in the first scripture to marry Gomer because "the people in this country have acted like prostitutes" and then, in this second scripture, He tells Hosea to continue after her because, "It is an example of the Lord's love for Israel." There was no other reason God wanted Hosea to marry this type of woman. It was not because God thought that Hosea was deeply in love with Gomer or that God felt like they were a perfect match for each other, or even that Hosea was looking for a person to marry. God strictly told Hosea to marry a prostitute for His only purpose and that was to show the relationship God had for His people, and the spiritual unfaithfulness that His people were continually displaying towards Him. God loved His people and when He delivered them from slavery and was bringing them to the Promised Land, they continued to be unfaithful to Him, not trusting Him wholeheartedly and worshipping other idols. But, God was faithful to His people that He loved so much. Hosea's purpose of this marriage was to give us perspective on how God loves. No other marriage that was joined by God in the Bible has representation like the marriage of Hosea. So, when choosing a mate today, never feel like God is telling you to choose someone who is mistreating you or that God is leading you to marry someone who is continually causing immense destructible heartache. That is not God's intention for you when selecting a mate. Hosea and Gomer was a match that only God put together for that one purpose. The demonstration was through Hosea, to show just how much God loved His people; to show God's grace and mercy towards His people; to show the redemption that took place for their disobedience.

Today, God does not have to match people like Hosea and Gomer to show His love for His people. He sent one person to show His love for us and that was Jesus Christ. Today, Jesus is the only person who, when we accept Him, we are able to experience God's grace, mercy, redemption, and the experience of His unfailing love. Hosea sacrificed to display God's love for His people, but Jesus Christ sacrificed the ultimate display of God's love for His people. So, when selecting a mate, you have a choice to select someone who God would want to join you to, or not. The choice is absolutely yours. If you do choose someone who God would not join you to, then yes, God can use you to win them over, but now that our Savior Jesus Christ lives within us, we are not ever led to marry someone who is not God's best for us. The Holy Spirit will always, always lead us in the right direction when choosing a mate. For some of us, we may miss that choosing because we do not rely on the Holy Spirit or God's wisdom when making that major decision of whom we should marry. If we do, there is always hope for redemption in the marriage; God will honor your faithfulness either way. But, you will be taking the longer road to oneness or even the odds against it when you choose what is not to follow God's best for you.

With this being said, it is clear I am stating that before being joined together, God intentionally made the husband to be whole in Him before a marriage was joined together. Why? This goes in hand with what He says about the roles of husbands loving their wives like Christ, and being the spiritual leader in the home. Husbands have to be that anchor, or rock, for the home, like Christ is for us. So, it is imperative that husbands are made whole before being joined to a wife.

Unfortunately, there are many marriages that are joined together erroneously, and nearly half of them end in divorce. I'm not trying to discourage you from marriage. But, what I am trying to say here is that many of them were not joined together by God. Many marriages are joined by our own fleshly desires, mostly because we really had no idea of what to look for in a spouse that would be considered God's best for us. There is a design that God has for marriages. When marriages are based on this design, the chances are higher of having a fulfilled marriage of completeness. Adam was complete in the image of God and through Adam; Eve was made complete in the image of God. Your completeness is in Christ always, but when it comes to being joined with someone, it's hard to be complete without the holy matrimony. We were all designed to desire a relationship with God; all of us, whether we want to admit it or not. So, when you decide to marry someone who is not whole in Christ, reaching the fulfillment of the holy matrimonial trinity that God designed can become more of a challenge. I will not go into the details of the holy matrimonial trinity here, because it can be read in the first book of this, *Us Against the World*, book series. But, in a nutshell, here is what the holy matrimonial trinity means.

```
        ⊙                          ⊙
    The Father                   Christ


  Jesus        Holy Spirit     Husband      Wife
  Christ       The Helper      Christ-      Helper
                               like         Holy
                                            Spirit-like
            │                          │
            ▼                          ▼
```

Holy Trinity/	Holy Matrimony/Man,
Three persons, one	Woman, Christ to
God in Unity	oneness in unity

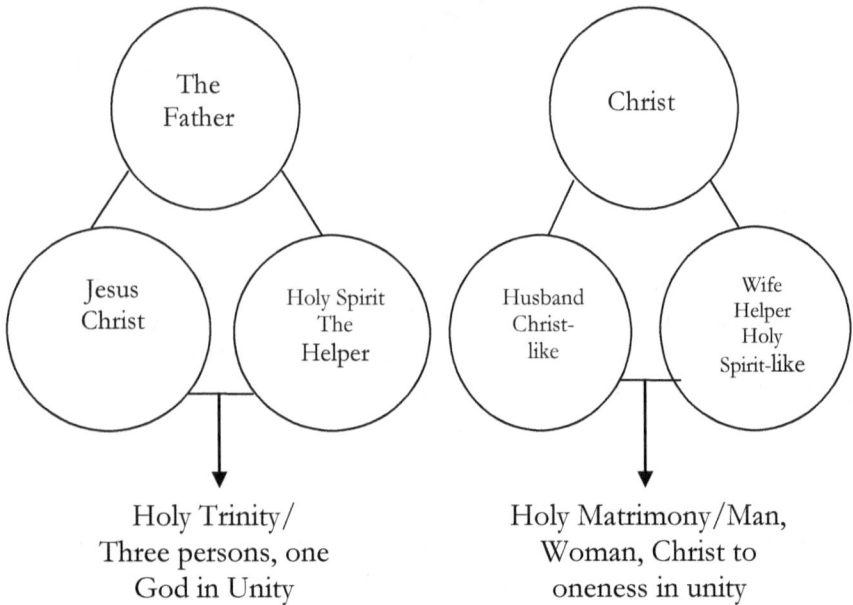

God designed for the husbands to be Christ-like, for husbands to love like Christ loves the church. The wives were designed to be the helper. There is only one other person in the Bible that is labeled the *Helper* and that is the Holy Spirit. So, the wife was designed to *be Holy-Sprit like*. But, both are to submit unto the Lord. When they are both in this design of oneness, then it makes the God designed holy matrimony complete. Does it guarantee that the marriage will be forever after? Well, is the Holy Trinity guaranteed to last forever? Yes! So, if God designed for the holy matrimony to be similar to the Holy Trinity, then yes, it was meant to last forever, so long as you both shall live. Really think about that statement. God has purpose for everything and His purposes are all for good, never for harm. So, if the marriage is Christ-centered, then husbands will love like Christ and wives will guide and encourage like the Holy Spirit. With a marriage trinity like that, a marriage can last forever. A marriage can overcome the obstacles that will come against them.

The reality of this message is that many of us have been or are in a relationship where only one or neither of us is whole in Christ. Truth is, we often get married pre-maturely whole in Christ and it takes years into our marriage before we realize that God's design is the best way before we become that holy matrimony that He initially designed. During that time of becoming the oneness that God designed, many of us get weary in doing so and become discouraged. This is not to say that even if you are joined whole in Christ then you will be in complete bliss and have all the answers of making it work. But, what it does mean is that when you are joined together and you are both whole in Christ, then you can work together through any storms that come up against you, because your holy matrimony will have the same mindset of how the Godhead Trinity works.

Earlier, I mentioned that God would not join a woman to a man who was not whole in Christ and that if we do join with someone who is outside of what God would join together, then it was our own doing out of our own flesh. This is why it is so important to truly understand what love really is and God has shown us exactly what that love looks like. People are drawn to people for many reasons, but in the end, it is imperative to rely on the Holy Spirit to guide you to the person God would join you with. The Holy Spirit will always guide you to do the right thing. You just have to trust that when you ask God to show you if the one you are with is from Him, that He will reveal it to you. Be patient and really pay attention when He is speaking to you.

For many of us, we get into a relationship and believe that the person we are with is the best for us, not realizing that God has His best for us. How do we know? Well, if you have to convince yourself why you think this person is the best for you and say things like, "He might not show it all the time, but I know he loves me;" "She's not that bad, but she'll change over time;" "He may not be romantic, but he has a good heart in there somewhere;" "She is not my dream woman, but no one else will take me;" or one that is often said most, "He may not go to church, pray, or read the Bible, but he is a Christian." I am going to repeat this, if you absolutely have to convince yourself and give reasons why you think this person is best for you, then it is not God's best for you. You should be marrying a person exactly for who they are and not what you think they can be. If you also have to give the person you are engaged with an ultimatum to being whole in Christ, then they are not God's best for you. I'm not saying that you will get this overwhelming sense of rainbows when you are together, and stars twirling around your heads as you walk through the sunset to know when a person is God's best for you. But, the key to knowing what God's best for you is knowing who God is and knowing who you are in Christ. God is all good and there is nothing in Him that is bad. God is also gracious, so if He is good and gracious, then He would not pair you up with someone who does not bring out the best in you.

God gave us personality traits, talents, gifts, dreams, and the ability to love one another. So, when He pairs us with someone, then His choice for us works out for the best in us and through us. You are highly valued by God and He sees you as precious to Him, so if you are precious and valuable to Him, how much more do you believe He would want to pair you up with someone who would see the same thing in you? Think of it this way, our earthly parents have an idea of the type of mate we should choose when selecting a lifetime partner. They may not know everything about your potential spouse, but they truly know what is best for you. So, they would not want to see us choose someone who is not going to be good for us. Our Heavenly Father feels the same way, but the difference is He knows everything about you and your potential spouse. So, you better believe He knows who is best for you; why not trust Him to help you choose a lifetime mate?

When you wholeheartedly seek for His face in your decision to marry a person, He will show you things that will let you know you are making the right decision. But, He will also show you some red flags if who you are considering is not His best for you. Pay very close attention to the red flags, because that is God speaking to you. When I first met the man that I married, I had just given my life to Christ, but I did not know how to rely on the Holy Spirit to help me know if he was "the one" and vice versa. In fact, we had no wisdom at all to know that God gave us specific guidelines when choosing a mate for life. There was something that did not feel right, but in my own flesh, I just wanted to get married. He did some things that were very hurtful and outside of the norm that I would have chosen in a person, but I was young and immature and have no real pinpoint reason why I still remained with him. There were red flags that I now see was something I should have paid attention to. I was not exactly an angel either and do not believe I was best for Him, either. After being married to him for nineteen years, I realized how deeply we hurt each other and how I suppressed so much of the pain and hid it in my heart. I went on year after year not realizing just how much damage had been done from his actions and my reactions to him. Also, how much I was traumatized until I began to go to a counselor. It took a counselor to bring out everything emotionally, but in the end, I knew it was all God bringing everything that was in the dark to light.

Throughout my process, I began to see things in the past and I saw all the ways that God was trying to warn us about marrying each other and I did not realize they were warnings from Him. When I started to see all the mistakes I made and all the things that I did to try and make this marriage work, I began to feel hopeless, because it had been exposed that the marriage I was in was not joined by God, but by our own fleshly desires. There was abuse, adultery, neglect, manipulation, idolization, spirit of mammon, and so much more, yet I kept trusting God that He would move in this marriage. Through His grace, I received the best kids He could ever give me and He did keep me in this marriage trusting Him. I did realize that my wholeness was only in God, not my husband. But, after living so many years with some lack, God made me realize the most important thing, and that was who He was and how much He truly valued me.

Once everything was exposed and we realized that there were biblical grounds to end the marriage, I had a very tough decision to make. Did I want to continue to be in a marriage where we did not value each other the way God did, or did I want to end it and experience God on an entire new level of forgiveness, grace, mercy, and the compassion He had for us as individuals? I could not choose for my spouse, but I did choose for myself, and I chose God. It was hard to make that decision because I am all about trusting God to make your marriage work, even if the other spouse is not everything you need to make a marriage work. I trusted God for nineteen years to fulfill both of us in our marriage, but we just never reached that point, because of all the damage that took place in our marriage, on both our parts. We did not have a fully *Christ-centered* marriage. Ultimately, it is still a choice, no matter how much you pray for a person to be in God's will. The person you are praying for has free will and unfortunately, if they choose to continue in their own will, then God will not cross that line, unless He is invited. So, I took the fork in the road as an opportunity to trust God to heal my heart from all the damage that took place in our marriage and to trust Him that His grace and mercy would help get me through my decision to leave. And to experience His love the way I never experienced so intimately before, but also trusted that God would work in the man I married, too, even if it meant being separated leading to divorce.

Why am I telling you this story? Again, not to discourage you, but to share my experience of the hard road we took when we said, "I do," and not truly waiting on God's best for each other in His own timing. We rushed into the marriage and we did it lacking God's wisdom. We were not equipped to handle our situations like the Godhead Trinity. I do believe that had we started off understanding the matrimonial trinity that God designed and that we were led to one another by the Holy Spirit, then our marriage would have been very strong today. We would have been able to make each other complete and even overcome the obstacles that took place in our marriage, even if they were biblical grounds for divorce.

I have, in the past, regretted not knowing that God had a *best* for me when it came to looking for a long-term mate. I was angry and unforgiving of myself for not understanding that and I felt like I was being punished for not heeding to His warning signs that He was trying to give me before deciding to say, "I do." But, God had to stop me from feeling that way and had to remind me that He forgave me over two-thousand years ago and He was not punishing me for the decision I made long ago. Yes, there were grounds for separation and it was painful to realize the truth, but God showed me a love that made me realize that I never want to go throughout life again without having His best for me. I don't want to settle for anything that is less than His best for anything in my life, and He does not want that for the man I married, either.

I do look back and believe had I really paid attention to the detrimental and obvious red flags, we would not have married. However, I can say it was because of my lack of wisdom and rushing into a marriage that I now have the compassion for people who are in relationships where they are just settling and not waiting on God's best. It hurts to see so many people in relationships where they have no idea of what God would want them to have and in relationships where they are not valued the way God values them. So, before you decide to tie the knot, ask yourself these hard reflection questions. But, these questions are to be answered just by you and not shared with your mate.

Reflection Questions:

Question 1: How does God value me? Does the person I am with value me in the same manner?

Question 2: Is the person I am with who God would want me to be joined with? List why you think so and list why you don't think so. Which ones align with God's guidelines and design for holy matrimony?

Question 3: Would you be willing to stay in the relationship forever if it is not what God would join together? Why or why not?

Chapter 4

Against God's Holy Matrimony Design

$\mathcal{S}$aying there is a certain design God has for marriage and that it is His best, is a very strong statement. I am by no means saying that a marriage can ONLY last if the marriage starts off this way. There are many marriages where they did not have a clue of the design and God turned their marriage around, so they can become that oneness He intends for couples to become so they can last forever. In other words, there is redemption when a marriage did not start off in HOLY matrimony. But, in all honesty, the only one who can keep the holy matrimony from not lasting forever is you. Even if we are in the design that God created for marriage, it is our flesh that can ruin it. So is the case with Adam and Eve. They were completely made whole and in the image of God, but they did not have their armor of God up and did not keep God at the center of their test and trial. When I first thought deeply about their story, I kind of wanted to give them the benefit of the doubt. They had no idea who Satan was, they had no idea that they could be deceived, manipulated, or fall into a trap. So, I asked why they would be held accountable for deception, if they knew no evil.

The serpent was the first type of evil they ever encountered. But, then it was made very clear to me, it is not whether or not they knew no evil, but it was because God had clear instructions and they were to follow them. He did not explain anything to them other than the fact that they were not to eat from the designated tree or they would die. That was clear instruction and all they had to do was follow His instruction. Their story made me realize that if God says to do something, then just trust that it is for your own good. If they would have continued to stand on the command that God gave them, then they would have been living and living life more abundantly together as a couple. But, their disobedience caused them a sentence that led them to spiritual death and eventually, physical death. Likewise, God gives a specific design of how we should love each other as husbands and wives. We don't know why He has the specifications of the design, but we can just trust it and believe it is for our own good while being married. If we don't trust what He says, and ask Him to help us live in His design, then the marriage can lead to spiritual death and eventually, the death of the marriage.

For those of you who are already in a relationship that seems it will start off in the holy matrimony that God intended, then you are already on a great path. It will not be perfect, but it will be easier than those who are not on that path. I say it will not be perfect, because just like Adam and Eve who were whole and who were made in the image of God, they still had their weaknesses and their fleshly desires. It was their own desires that caused them to fall in their union, and they had a severe consequence from their fall. However, even though they fell, they still looked to the Lord for help.

"Adam made love to his wife Eve, and she became pregnant and gave birth to Cain. She said, "With the help of the LORD I have brought forth a man."

(Genesis 4:1, NIV)

This scripture pertains to being blessed with a child by God's help, but it also shows that they still relied upon God for help. It could indicate that even though the Lord told them to multiply, they may have had the challenges of multiplying before the challenges they had through their kids, but they relied on God and His grace was still there for them. Likewise, you will have challenges, but if you are in God's design for holy matrimony, then it's His grace, and the grace within you, that can get you through the challenges.

For those of you who are currently in a relationship that does not seem like it will start off in the holy matrimonial design God intended, then you have to decide whether or not you are willing to settle for less than God's best, and pray that it will one day become the way God initially designed. If you decide to continue in a relationship that you know is not necessarily God's best for you, then be prepared to take on more. It will take more work than you know, and you will have to go through some serious challenges. When you go through those challenges, it will be harder to deal with them when you are not on the same page as the holy matrimony God designed. One of you will desire so much of God's wisdom in marriage, while the other will have no clue of what that means. There will be many days when you are on your knees praying for your marriage, and it will seem like you are the only one fighting for your marriage. It's called a *one-way* marriage, or being *unequally yoked.*

"Do not be unequally yoked with unbelievers. For what partnership has righteousness with lawlessness? Or what fellowship has light with darkness."

(2 Corinthians 6:14, NIV)

A one-way marriage is when one of you is *light* and one of you is *dark*, when one of you is *righteous* in Christ and the other is living *worldly*, when one of you *trusts and believes in our Savior* and the other one *trusts in self or other means*. A one-way marriage is when one of you is fighting through God's grace and the other is fighting through own might. Think of it this way, in parts of some countries, farmers still use a set of oxen to plow their crop. A set of oxen are paired together with a yoke, or a wooden bar, in order to work togeth-er equally and carry the loads in unity. However, if one oxen is shorter than the other, stronger than the other, taller than the other, or bigger than the other, then one will carry the load more than the other, and their work will be in opposition with one another. This will delay the end result or maybe become incomplete, because of the inadequa-cy of the two. However, when both oxen are securely matched with a yoke, then plowing will be easier, and the end result will be a good crop with a fulfilling harvest.

So, when two people are not equally yoked, then reaching the oneness that God initially designed for couples to reach will be very difficult. If one has a different philosophical view over the other, then it will cause conflict, strife, resistance, hostility, and unbearable disagreements.

I'm not saying that it is impossible; I am saying that it can become a long, uphill, drawn out battle. It can sometimes feel like something is missing, or a lack of connection with one another.

When I married the man I was with, it started off with distrust and insecurity. I realized very quickly that I needed God's hand in our marriage. I needed help to stick to my marriage vows. For years, I prayed that God would make some changes in our marriage. He did make some changes, but because our marriage was not based upon the God-designed holy matrimony, it always still felt empty to me. God did bless me with many other things that were connected to being married, but I never felt a real connection to my spouse. I was not complete in my marriage and as much as I prayed and believed, something was just not right. Over time, I got weary and simply accepted what I could not change, and just appreciated everything else that God blessed me with. I finally realized what was not right and it was because Christ was not completely the center of our marriage. He was not fully the Lord over our marriage and it was a difficult one-way marriage. But, I was still blessed with some of God's other best things for my life, like my kids, being a stay-at-home-mom, and the ability to have an amazing adventure with them. It was His grace that blessed me with those things and what helped me to stay in a half-truth, one-way marriage for so long. The damage that was done in our marriage was overshadowed with those blessings and I was coping.

When we started to go to counseling that is when things started to really unravel in my marriage. I started to see how we were so une-qually yoked and how because of our different views, why we could not reach the fulfillment of oneness. There was so much damage in our marriage that happened throughout the years, but the coping mechanisms I was using to get past the hurts and pains we were causing each other were wearing off. After they wore off, it was like the mud had just been lifted off my eyes, so that I could see the truth of the matter. Our marriage was dead. The abuse, the infidelity, and the lack of understanding the vital importance of a *Christ-centered* marriage revealed why our marriage was so empty. It revealed why we never were able to reach the oneness that God desired for us. Had we both been on board of having a *Christ-centered* marriage, then I truly believe that even though we had biblical grounds for separating, we would have been able to overcome the obstacles that damaged us in a healthier and prospering way.

I've had people ask me to explain what being unequally yoked means. The oxen example pretty much explains it, but being unequally yoked means exactly what the scripture says. In a partnership, it's hard to connect with one another when one is living in righteousness under Christ and one is living under lawlessness. One who follows the Word of God and one who does not. One who is Christ-like minded and one who is carnally-minded. It is hard to fellowship with one who is in darkness, while the other is shining in light. One who lives in freedom from sin and one who is in bondage to sin. One who lives in truth and one who is deceptive. Being unequally yoked can be a major challenge in a relationship, and eventually, it will lead one to the other side of the unequal spectrum.

I have several friends who are Believers; some, who are divorced, some who are single, and some who are married. At some point of our friendship, the discussion came up about how it is important to be in a relationship with a Believer. Through experiences, we all realized how hard it is to be with someone who is not a Believer. So, there was that determination not to be with someone who was not a Believer. However, throughout the years, they have fallen for someone who may have or may not have been a Christian, and still lived carnally-minded. The thing about selecting a person is that, sure, they can say they are a Christian, but not live in the Holy Spirit and by the Word of God. Soon after being in a relationship with the unbeliever or the one who claimed themselves as a "Christian," who was carnally-minded, they found themselves not going to church, because their partner wasn't going, they stopped reading the Bible for themselves, they stopped praying, and they stopped worshipping and praising. They were pulled into the lawlessness, or the darkness, by the other. The good thing is that the light and righteousness will eventually be greater than the darkness, but what happens is they wasted a time in their life where they were stagnant before they realized the light within them. When they finally realized the value that God had in them, they wasted a period of time being with someone who led them into this deceiving place. Eventually, they had to make a decision and that was to continue being in this unequally yoked relationship, or work in prayer to win the carnally one to the light.

Many, who have been in a relationship like this, will choose to stay in it hoping and praying their significant other will come to the light. The good news is that many have won them over, or will win them over after a very long drawn out battle. Those who do not win them over have to realize that it is not hope and prayer that is not winning them over, it is the free-will within the other person that is keeping them from wanting to be won over.

Being committed to a marriage whether or not it is based on the foundation of God's design will naturally take work, but the more we go against His best for our marriage, the more grace and love it will take to stay in it and it can only be given to you through God. Our own flesh will make mistakes in the marriage over and over again, but without God, it will be more difficult to become that full *oneness* that God blesses couples to experience. So, when you are in an unequally yoked relationship, decide if you are willing to sacrifice and take that chance to become equally yoked. This can take many years or you can move from it and wait on someone who will be equally yoked with you from the start. Good news is that even in those relationships that are not equally yoked; it can be redeemed through Christ and can eventually reach the oneness that is desired by both. You just have to decide what you are willing to sacrifice in the relationship.

If you really want to know if you are in a relationship that is God's best for you, then ask Holy Spirit to identify it to you. God will reveal it and lead you to make the right decision. If you are ready to hear the truth and it is revealed that you are not in God's best, then it will not be easy for you to simply leave the relationship. You have feelings and emotions that are all tied up into it. It will be hard to free yourself from it right away. But, if you have asked Holy Spirit to guide you in this decision, then you have to believe that Holy Spirit will give you everything you need to walk away from it. It will certainly take lots of renewing your mind and His strength that will be made perfectly in your weakness. God knows that it will not be easy for you, but that is why He sent Holy Spirit to help you. Holy Spirit will gently guide you and will not give you more than you can bear to overcome the action of leaving the relationship.

Reflection Questions:

Question 1: Do you believe that you and your significant other are equally yoked or not? Explain.

Question 2: If you are equally yoked, what same philosophical views do you think you will need to use most to overcome obstacles? In contrast, if you are unequally yoked, how will you be able to overcome the obstacles that may arise in your relationship, and do you think over time it will continue to work?

Chapter 5

Against Pre-Marital Sex

*D*o you remember, as a young teen, you vowed that you would wait to have sex until you are married? Many teenage super-stars have vowed that publically, later to find out that they couldn't quite keep that vow after all. Why is it so hard to keep a vow of abstinence? Number one, because it is a strong temptation that the ruler of the world uses to reel you in to keep you in bondage to him. Number two, because it is a natural gift that God gave us, in order to connect. Sex is not just used to procreate, it is such a beautiful expression that God gave us to be able to connect with each other. Sex was meant to be a good thing for a couple, but Satan uses it to rob, kill, and destroy intimacy between us. So, the best way to see how it can attack you as an engaged couple is to first understand what sex is in God's eyes, and then see what sex is in Satan's eyes.

Sex through God's Eye

"For this is the will of God, even your sanctification, that ye should abstain from <u>fornication:</u> That every one of you should know how to possess his vessel in sanctification and honour; Not in the lust of <u>concupiscence,</u> even as the Gentiles which know not God."

(1 Thessalonians 4:3-5, KJV, emphasis)

The first way that God sees sex is that it is a *sanctification* and *holy* only for His purposes and not for our own lustful desires. His purposes are pure and honorable and when we are having sex for any other reason, then it does go against His will for what He designed its beauty. What's His purpose for sex? Well, the cut and dry purpose is for couples to experience sex in a most phenomenal way to bring emotions and intimacy together, as a joining to each other. Sex is such a wonderful experience, but He only intended it to be for married couples. He intended that couples experience sex in such a personal way that only they should be able to uniquely enjoy it. In addition to that joining of intimacy, God's other purpose is so that couples can procreate children. When two people are joined together in holy matrimony, God created sex so that they can have children in the likeness of their holy union. We discussed what the holy union looks like; husband, *Christ-like*; wife, *the helper, Holy-Spirit-like*; both under the leadership of Christ our Lord and Savior. When this holy matrimony takes place, then to God, it is the perfect timing of having children to reflect the extension of their union. To help explain this in detail, take a look at this scripture:

"Then God said, "Let us make mankind in our image, in our likeness, so that they may rule over the fish in the sea and the birds in the sky, over the livestock and all the wild animals, and over all the creatures that move along the ground."

So God created mankind in his own image, in the image of God he created them; male and female he created them.

God blessed them and said to them, "Be fruitful and increase in number; fill the earth and subdue it."

(Genesis 1:26-28, NIV)

When God said, "Let us make mankind in our image," who was He referring to? He was referring to Him the Godhead, the Holy Trinity, and He did not create mankind, until after He completed everything on earth first. When He sculpted and perfected everything on earth to His expression of it being *good*, that is when He decided to make mankind and the extension of His likeness and the goodness of who He was and always is.

As a couple, we want to form little beings that are an extension of who we are just like God did with Adam and Eve, who eventually fruitfully bore children to populate the earth and increase mankind in number. So, God wonderfully designed sex as a means of being able to accomplish this. He sees sex in marriage as the perfect timing to bear children. His perfect timing would be when husband and wife are whole in Christ and display the holy matrimony union in His image. He did not create mankind in His own image and likeness, until after His perfect work of the entire earth was complete, so ideally, the perfect timing to have children would be when husband and wife are in complete holy matrimony. Why, because then a husband and wife who are in holy matrimony under God can raise godly offspring. God desires for man and woman to raise their offspring under godly wisdom. This was the reason He joined two people to become one.

"But did He not make them one, Having a remnant of the Spirit? And why one? He seeks godly offspring."

(Malachi 2:15, NKJV)

The second way that God sees sex is an emotion that should be controlled. Sex is so powerful and once sex takes place between two people, it forms a bond, or a union, between the two. To fall into the temptation of sex is very easy, and to detach yourself from the bond created by sex is difficult. This bond stirs up all kinds of feelings and attraction to one another and if not careful, you could be bonding, or forming, a union with someone that is not God's best for you. So, He highly stresses the importance of controlling your urges and temptations for sex. In order to do that, you have to view your body as something precious to Him. God created you in His own image, so everything that makes up you is very important to Him, including your body. So, He wants you to honor your body and care for it in such a way that is honorable. I am not talking about making sure you don't get tattoos or that you should not have that tummy tuck. I am talking about saving sex for God's purposes. Sex is one of the joys and tools God is using so that two people in a marriage reach the fulfillment of *oneness.*

Sex through Satan's Eyes

"For everything in the world-the lust of the flesh, the lust of the eyes, and the pride of life-comes not from the Father but from the world."

(I John 2:16, NIV)

"The thief comes only to steal and kill and destroy; I have come that they may have life, and have it to the full."

(John 10:10, NIV)

In contrast to how God sees sex as a way to connect married couples with each other in a very personal and intimate way, Satan sees sex as a way to have lustful desires with each other. He uses sex to portray love and desire for one another, but his plans are to use it before marriage. Why is it so important for Satan to use it before marriage? He knows that sex can connect people together in such a powerful way that they can be in bondage to one another, leading in this false sense of what love really means. Instead of love, he uses it for two people to lust after each other and desire each other for the wrong reasons. Emotionally, sex can tie two people's souls together like no other way. For each person we are having sex with, we are giving a piece of ourselves to them and collecting a piece of them to ourselves. For some that we had sex with, we formed these emotional attachments that can hinder us from future healthier relationships, because we are so attached to this false perception of love from a past, actively sexual relationship. Sex can keep two people in bondage to each other when they know deep down that they are not in a relationship that is God's best for them.

In addition to these unhealthy pre-marital sexual relationships, Satan uses them to form broken families. Instead of creating an extension of little images of a husband and wife in holy matrimony, he uses sex to bore babies into unmarried homes. He uses the selfishness in people to have babies under unfortunate circumstances that cause poverty, kids living in single family homes, babies born in dependence of drugs, and babies not able to be fulfilled by loving and supportive parents who would be in agreement on how to raise children together. He also uses sex to create an illusion for married couples to have sexual desires for someone outside their marriage. However, that is covered in the first book on marriage in this book series. So, let's just concentrate on pre-marital sex. Of course, these are just a few ways that Satan uses sex for his purposes. Remember the thief's plan is to rob, kill, and destroy.

There is no doubt about it that you will be put in very tempting situations to want to have sex with each other. So, be very mindful when sex is becoming an opportunity in your relationship and really evaluate if it is for God's purposes or for fleshly desires for Satan's purposes. Make up in your mind that your relationship with God is more important than your fleshly desires.

Reflection Questions:

Question 1: How do you view sex while engaged? Do you both agree on it?

Question 2: If you choose to refrain from sex until married, what measures are you going to need to take to achieve this and how difficult will this be for you?

Question 3: Do you think sex would be a better experience before marriage or after? Explain.

Chapter 6

Against Idolizing the Marriage Institution

$\mathscr{I}$ was watching Iyanla Vanzant's: *Fix My Life* one day and it was a three part series on marriages that appeared beyond repair. One question that she asked the woman was did you marry the person, the promise, or the penis (it could be asked the same for men by replacing the p-word with the unorthodox female terminology). When she asked that question, it made me think about that for a moment. When we decide to tie the knot, what are we marrying? The *person*, the *promise* or the p-sexual organ? The ladies on the show all answered the *promise*. Not saying that it is a wrong answer, but I really had to think about that answer, and it made me realize that most will marry for that reason; the promise. I got something a little different than what was portrayed on the show, but it made me realize that if we marry the person, we are marrying the person for who they are, how they treat us, what their philosophical views are, their background, and everything else that makes up that person who we found to be marriage material. If we marry the *p-organ*, then we are marrying the passion and sexual chemistry that draws us to them. This leaves marrying the *promise*. The promise that we marry is the wedding vows and the commitment of marriage and the promise that it will last forever. However, when we get so caught up on marrying the promise of commitment to a marriage, we can consume the entire relationship on that promise and miss out on the type of person we should marry, or fall into the false sense of love with the *p-sexual organ*. Not only that, but we also fall into the idolizing of the marriage institution.

Think of it like this, little girls have these imaginative fantasies about what it would be like to marry and have this *princess-like* wedding. They started these imaginations when Barbie and Ken or the newest phase of dolls was introduced to them, or through playing house with friends. Getting married is a dream to come true for many little girls. While pretending to get married, the little girl doesn't exactly care what the little boy looks like or what he is about or not even thinking about acting on the "you may now kiss the bride" portion of their imagination; he is there and available to play along. For little boys, they did not necessarily start off with imagining a big wedding, but they did just kind of go along with the setting simply for fun. With this in mind, it's no surprise why they came out with T.V. shows such as, *Bridezilla*, or *Marriage at First Sight*. They focus so much on the wedding part of the marrying experience, hoping that it will be an everlasting commitment. Unfortunately, for some of us, the wedding expense can become outrageous and can start your marriage off in debt! But, getting married and having a wedding has become some sort of a factor that puts a seal of value in each other. The sad reality is after all the expense of getting married; some couples find themselves a couple or several years down the road wanting to divorce. Why is that? Did they marry the person, promise, or p-sexual organ?

There is absolutely nothing wrong with marrying the commitment or promise. It's what couples hope to achieve until the very end to live happily ever after. It's why you get engaged. But, you cannot have a satisfying commitment if you did not marry the right person, nor can you have it if you married out of sexual gratification. The institution of marriage is definitely a gift from God, because He knows that many of us desire to have that type of commitment. But, sometimes, what can happen is we replace the gift of marriage or the desire to marry that God has given to us as some form of *god* or we *idolize* it. When we start to idolize it, then it becomes more important than God, and we miss out on the best relationship of all in Him. We begin to think that who we marry will be the one who completes us. We also sometimes believe that marriage is an ultimate destination that God is bringing us to. That is not the case, marriage is simply a blessing that God gives to those who desire it, but when we desire it for our own selfish reasons and do not see it as an added blessing that God gives us, then we start to rely on it for our happiness. For those already married who idolize marriage, the focus becomes on trying to keep it together for the rest of their lives and never become fulfilled by it. When people start to idolize their marriage, they can put God on the back burner and start losing who they are as an individual, feeling incomplete.

"And ye are complete in him, which is the head of all principality and power:"

(Colossians 2:10, NIV)

God makes it clear that we are not complete in man, but in Him. When we are complete in God, then everything else becomes blessings we receive from Him. Not only blessings from Him, but we come to know these blessings as beautiful journeys; journeys that He is head of and that we trust Him to make fulfilling. This is how we should see marriage; a beautiful journey in which God wants you to have in fulfillment, but only through Him in His perfect will. When we start to put the idea of marriage, or marriage itself, as our happiness, then it blinds us from making the right decisions that God would want for us.

During my young adult years, I was focused on going to college and completing it. I had hopes to become a licensed counselor after college. While in college, I was dating and had some pretty good relationships and some not so good. But, I had a strong desire to also meet someone who I was going to marry. After some bad experiences with relationships, I met this one guy who all he had to say was that he wanted to marry me and I took it. I was so focused on the fact that he wanted a commitment with me for life, that I had no focus on whether or not we were compatible or equally yoked. We were both young and had so much baggage as individuals, but did not realize what we were bringing into the relationship. Those baggage issues we had were very unhealthy, but at that time, I had the fantasy that the *promise* would keep us together.

Before the marriage, the baggage issues were visible, but ignored by ignorance. After we got married, the baggage issues became hurtful issues in our marriage and caused some major damage to our well-being, particularly mine. He, at the time, was an abusive man and an unfaithful husband who had multiple affairs. At that time, I had a controlling and a judgmental spirit. Since I was so committed to our vows or the promise we made, I did seek for advice that I hoped would be beneficial for both of us while married, but the advice given was to just stick to the marriage vows, because they were made before God. I was given scriptures to follow and stand on to pray for the man I married, and even given scriptures that taught me to simply deal, because that is what I had to do as a wife. However, I was not ever given advice to help me understand the value of who I was in Christ, nor was I given Scripture to guide me into making wiser decisions to help me heal. So, the advice that was given to me was based upon just keeping the "promise" that was made, no matter what the cost.

I kept living the way I was taught in order to keep the promise of the marriage institution. The scriptures I prayed out of legalism were just to stand on my promise as a married couple. It became the main focus of my prayer life. I idolized and cherished the marriage institution, or the promise. The scriptures that I focused on were that God would change my husband to love me like Christ and that God would help me to have a quiet spirit and submit to my husband. This was the perfect couple taught to me, in order to have a promising marriage. If I just prayed on this, then we would become the ideal of a marriage institution. So, year after year, I stood on these scriptures believing we were going to become that husband and wife to make the marriage institution perfect. While I prayed this year after year, I could not understand why we could not reach the end result.

It was revealed to me that I valued the marriage institution more than the relationship that God desired with me. I made my then husband and our marriage a determination to change, so I could be happy. While I thought I was being a good *Christian wife* and doing the right thing to fight for my marriage, I did not realize that I was replacing it with my relationship with God. God has always desired a very personal relationship with me, as He does with everyone, so that He could help me heal past the hurts, help me see things the way that He saw things, and to help me personally hear from Him to seek direction in my life. But, because I was so focused on the legalistic aspects of scriptures and applying it to my marriage based on what other people said, I missed out on a very personal and intimate relationship with what God desired for me. Because I missed this personal relationship with Him, I made some very unwise decisions just hoping He would change them to make them better. He did in some ways, but what I had to eventually realize is that no matter how much I prayed using those scriptures, we both had to be complete in Him for those changes to take place. Neither one of us understood this scripture on how we are made complete in Christ. I unintentionally idolized my marriage over real completeness in Christ.

I have been a Christian since I was seventeen, but unfortunately, I was a very late bloomer in understanding what that really meant. When I finally understood what being complete in God meant, that is when my reality was revealed about my marriage. I believe that had I established a very personal relationship with Christ before marrying and even earlier in my marriage, I would have not just married for a promise, nor would I have focused on keeping a marriage institution under legalistic terms, but more so with an understanding of what God would have wanted for me, because of who He is. When making a decision to marry, don't let the promise be your motivating factor. As I said earlier, there is nothing wrong with marrying the promise, but in order to have a fulfilling promise for your marriage, you must first have a personal relationship with God that will allow you to choose the best person for you. Having the best person for you will allow you to overcome the obstacles that might try to come against your marriage institution, as well as helping you overcome the obstacles in your marriage will allow you to enjoy the intimacy in ways that only God intended for you to enjoy with your mate. Just remember that marriage is an added blessing to your life and not a crutch to your happiness.

Reflection Questions:

Question 1: Why do you want to get married? First, list the reason why you want to get married without mentioning your mate. Then, list why you want to marry the mate you chose.

Question 2: What does it mean that you are complete in Christ?

Chapter 7

Against Baggage

*W*e all know that it is our families, circumstances, and connections that we had growing up that shape and mold us to whom we become as an adult. There are some good things that have shaped us to have great character, good morals, values, and work ethics that become very beneficial in our marriages. However, in addition to those things that shape and mold us, we also have experiences. Those experiences can be positive and motivate us to share them with others, but experiences can also be negative and leave a bad taste in our mouth. Sometimes bad experiences can help us change things that need to be changed, but it's when those bad experiences have not been dealt with before hand and brought into a relationship that can become poisonous. They are the baggage from the past that we carry with us into our relationships that get in the way of connecting in a healthy manner.

Everyone has some kind of baggage, some heavier than others. Some examples of baggage are some form of abuse, an unforgiving spirit, past dysfunctional relationships, past failures, regrets, and generational behaviors like substance abuse or violence. Oftentimes, people do not know that they are bringing baggage into their relationships because they have no idea how their baggage will effect someone else. Their baggage becomes their norm of living and it is not often revealed on how much it is affecting their relationships until years later.

I love this song by Erykah Badu, called *Bag Lady*. The lyrics, of course, were meant for the many women who carry baggage, which you can read, but keep in mind, I cut out the repetition of some parts of the song.

Catherine Harmon

Bag lady, you gon' hurt your back

Draggin' all them bags like that

I guess nobody ever told you

All you must hold on to is you, is you, is you

One day all them bags gon' get in your way

So pack light

Bag lady you gon' miss your bus

You can't hurry up 'cos you've got too much stuff

When they see you coming they just take off running

From you, it's true, oh yes they do

One day he gon' say you crowding my space

So pack light

Girl I know

Sometimes it's hard and we can't let go

If someone hurts you oh so bad inside

You can't deny it, you can't stop crying

116

So if you start breathing then you won't believe it

You'll feel so much better, so much better baby

So where my garbage bag lady

And what about the grocery bag lady

I'm talkin' to my Gucci bag ladies

And what about my paper sack ladies

What about my nickel bag ladies

Light pack when ya pack ya bags ladies

And what about my… bag ladies

And what about the cheap sack babies

So what about the plastic bag ladies

And my baby baggin' mamas

All my book bag ladies

Zip-lock bag ladies

Let it go, let it go, let it go, let it go

The reason why I love this song so much is because the song writer shows the reflection of how women carry baggage into relationships and do not always know how to let the loads go. Then, she goes on to list the different types of bag ladies. However, this is also a reflection of how any one of us, both male and female, can carry baggage into our relationships that can eventually break our backs and destroy our relationships if we don't deal with them, so we can let them go.

It's a secular song, but it brings a little bit of meaning to this chapter. When you think about this song, think about the baggage you may be bringing into your relationship. Loads after loads can weigh you down to the point where it slows down your progress in your relationship's growth.

On the other hand, think about the baggage your mate has and how it is affecting you. When you are willing to pick up someone who has too much baggage, then their baggage becomes your baggage. You may already have your own baggage, but then to have to pick up someone else's, too, when yours has not been put down yet can start weighing you down, as well. It becomes this cycle of throwing each other's baggage on each other. Then, their baggage becomes magnified and it gets in the way of your happiness. It can become a toxic relationship.

It's easy to point out your mate's baggage that they may be bringing in, but not always easy recognizing your own baggage. When you can get to a place where you can actually recognize the baggage you are bringing into your relationship, then you can start letting go. The best thing you can do before you walk down that aisle is evaluate any baggage that you need to leave at the bus stop before getting on the ride. You should do this with a counselor. In this century, the importance of pre-marital counseling is strongly advised, and during this time of counseling, really use it to talk about the baggage you are bringing into the marriage and identify it. It might be painful and it might stir up some old feelings, but it will be so worth unloading it, so that you can deal with it and move forward to a healthy relationship. In addition to counseling, it is most important to let go of the baggage through prayer.

"Casting all your care upon him; for he careth for you."

(Peter 5:7, KJV)

God knows the depths of your heart. Your heart is like a little treasure box to Him. He has every keepsake in the box from the time you were born until eternity. He knows every joy and every pain that you have. He wants to get rid of any pains that are in your heart, so that you can live victoriously, peacefully, and joyously. When you cast any of the pains, regrets, past relationships, etc. on Him, He can help you heal from them or change your viewpoints on them. He will help you renew your mind, so that when you go into your relationship, you can go with new beginnings for this new journey

"Do not conform to the pattern of this world, but be transformed by the renewing of your mind. Then you will be able to test and approve what God's will is--his good, pleasing and perfect will."

(Romans 12:12, NIV)

Reflection Questions:

Question 1: Is there anything that your mate does not know about you that you have not disclosed yet? If so, why haven't you disclosed it?

Question 2: What type of baggage do you see that your mate has that might affect your relationship in the long run?

Question 3: Are you willing to get counseling for the possible baggage that may affect your relationship before getting married? Why or why not?

Chapter 8

Against Finances

$\mathcal{M}$oney... is one of the greatest causes of problems in a marriage. There are several issues where money causes a strain in marriage and none of them can be resolved if you both are not on the same page with the handling of finances. Mishandling is a huge issue. Let's look at some of the main causes why money is such a problem in a marriage.

Merging of Money

Merging money after marriage is a big step and many couples will question themselves if they are ready to do that. To be able to merge money requires complete trust in each other and it requires you to be transparent. If you made a choice to marry your spouse, then at some point, the characteristic of trust-worthiness in money and being able to be transparent with each other may have already been observed before saying, *I do*, right? If so, then merging money should not be an issue. However, in many marriages, it is a huge issue and it is not understood how it can benefit the marriage.

"That is why a man leaves his father and mother and is united to his wife, and they become one flesh."

(Genesis 2:24, NIV)

Flesh is an important function in the body and although some parts of the body care for other parts of the body (example: eye lids protect the bulbus oculi or eyeball, the heart pumps blood through the blood vessels, or the brain signals the body's actions), it all still works together to care for one body, as a whole. God makes it clear that you are to become **one** flesh when you marry. He did not say to become flesh connecting to each other or flesh in just certain areas. Every area of your two different lives should become one and work together as one, in order to care for one another. You are to come together and act as one spiritually, emotionally, intimately, intellectually, and yes, this includes financially. So, for those of you who are having a hard time even thinking about merging your finances, what is it that is keeping you from making that decision?

The world says you should have separate accounts, because you should not depend on each other and instead, be self-sufficient. Every husband and every wife should either be delegated to certain bills in the house or they should just split the bills down the middle. The rest of the money can be spent on whatever it is they want for their own pleasure. The thing about this is that you are not roommates, you are a married couple. The definition of self-sufficiency is needing no outside help in satisfying one's basic needs; emotionally and intellectually independent (Oxford dictionary). So, why get married if you need self-sufficiency? Marriage was not designed for self-sufficiency. It is a joining of two people to live a life together. That life includes living under one roof to call home, so that you can build a stable future for your dreams of careers, children, and fulfillment in each other. You could not do that successfully being self-sufficient in two separate homes.

To go even further, God commands a husband to leave his father and mother and unite with his wife. He does not command the woman to leave her mother and father to unite with her husband. Although, it is clear that they should be uniting together regardless. The reason for this command is because God has a plan for each unity of marriage and He has a specific purpose for it. But, before He can fully work in the unity, a husband must separate from his parents and attach to his wife. A father and a mother provide everything that their child needs, emotionally, spiritually, physically, intellectually, and financially. The child is fully dependent upon their parents, but when the child becomes an adult and decides to marry, they are to become responsible for their own family. A husband, in particular, should be protecting, providing, and pasturing his family. Providing requires him to be stable in his income and ensuring that he is caring to meet his family's needs financially. A husband can fulfill his part as scripture says, but God goes a step further and adds that they should become one flesh. That seals the command that a husband should merge the finances, in order to accomplish one of the many goals God has for that unity.

There are many people who counter against this, and I say that if you, as a couple, decide to have separate accounts, then by all means, this is your choice and you may have good reasons for it. But, I also just want to point out the benefits of joining together. There are great benefits when couples merge their finances. The first benefit is *trust*. Merging allows each partner to know what amount is coming in and what bills need to be taken care of. The next benefit is *future planning*. After establishing what is coming in and what is going out, it gives couples a sense of where they stand and what they need to do to start preparing for a more secure future. It is good to be on one accord with finances also, because let's say one of the spouses gets really sick or dies, you will have been established to know where the finances stand and can move forward from there. The last benefit is that it *makes things easier*. With both of you being on the same page, there will not be any confusion as to who owes what or what account it will come out of. You will both know what needs to be taken care of, when, and how much. Simplicity.

Secret Money Accounts

Having secret accounts can be hurtful and deceiving, especially if it is later discovered by the unknowing spouse. The world tells husbands and wives to make sure they have a secret account, just in case the other wants to divorce. The world tells us that because divorce seems to be a stronger possibility to happen. It is the sad truth that divorce rates are extremely high and because of all the sinful possibilities, people want to be prepared for divorce. But, since God has already established that couples must become one in every area of their life, including finances, then having a secret account goes against His command. When a spouse takes action to stash money away secretly, then it means two things: they do not trust their spouse and they do not trust God. God does not want you to go into a marriage with the presumption, or the fear, that it can end in divorce. He wants you to go into the marriage believing that you are marrying the one person you are going to spend the rest of your life with, putting all your trust in Him concerning it.

"Overhearing what they said, Jesus told him, "Don't be afraid; just believe."

(Mark 5:36, NIV)

You are probably thinking that there is no harm in preparing yourself just in case the one you are marrying will let you down. It is not about the harm, it is still about trusting in God. Go into the marriage believing and expecting that you will victoriously stay in the marriage until death do you part with God's love to help conquer it. However, if it does ever come to a point where your spouse does let you down and a divorce was not what you wanted, your secret stash is not what you should trust in; it is God that you should trust. There will be no need for a secret stash if God is your provider. God does not like divorce, but He will not let you down if your spouse walks out on you, or if you leave because of infidelity. He will be on your side to help you become self-sufficient from your spouse. Trust in only Him and not a secret stash. If a stash is what you need, then at least be open and honest with your spouse and let them know it is something you would like to do. Discuss it and come to an agreement that it will be okay with the understanding of why. That is no different than telling them you would like a prenuptial. You are at least honest about it.

"But blessed is the one who trusts in the LORD, whose confidence is in him."

(Jeremiah 17:7, NIV)

Other reasons why spouses may have secret money are because they have secret addictions like gambling or financial trading. Maybe, they have secret money so they can spend more on their hobbies or spend more on shopping, than they are willing to let the spouse know about. Whatever the reason is, God did not intend it to be that way and it can almost be viewed as some form of embezzlement in the marriage.

Outrageous Amounts of Debt

For some couples, they are already starting their marriage off in debt by planning for an extravagant and beautiful wedding. Go figure. However, other debt may have been created apart from the wedding and if not researched ahead of time, you can marry someone who has more debt than you do. If that is the case, then oftentimes, the worldliness in the other spouse does not think they should be responsible for the other's debt. Not true. Since you will be in a marriage together, then you should pay it off together. It will be part of your vow. Let's refresh some memories on the traditional vows that are typically said at weddings.

"I, [your name], take you [spouse name], to be my [husband/wife], to have and to hold from this day forward; for better or for worse; **for richer, for poorer**; in sickness and in health; to love and to cherish from this day forward until death do us part"

"It is better not to make a vow than to make one and not fulfill it."

(Ecclesiastes 5:4, NIV)

Before saying, *I do*, you have plenty of time to research each other and discover each other's spending habits, borrowed loans, credit card spending, etc. This is information that could be discussed before making plans for a wedding, or information that could be observed. If you do not condition yourselves to take care of your debts before marrying, then saying, *I do* means you are both ready to incur a debt that you may or may not have created together, and are willing to handle it *for richer or for poorer*. It is one of the unpleasant vows to fulfill, but committing to it is preparing you to open up room for blessings later. So, please go over your finances before saying *I do*, so you can come into agreement on how to pay the debts off.

125

Most couples go into more debt by getting loans for a house, cars, and running up credit cards. The world says that you should have a four bedroom, three baths, two car garage house with a picket fence, two cars, at least two children, and a dog. There is nothing wrong with getting loans to have these things, as long as you can pay them back. But, sometimes, couples get into these debts too quickly, and they dream big before slowly preparing for it. This causes a major financial strain on the marriage. God does not want us in debt.

"The rich rule over the poor, and the borrower is slave to the lender."

(Proverbs 22:7, NIV)

We become slaves to the very people, or institution, we borrow from. Some for a lifetime! So, be very careful when selecting for what loans you need, versus for what you want. The world dictates what is considered a nicer home to have, a nicer car to drive, what latest technology to use, and what fabulous brand name clothes to wear. There is nothing wrong with wanting all the things the world says is "better;" however, be wise and shop smart. Shop for what is feasible during the current time in your life. If you have to start off in an apartment while you are waiting to climb up the promotional ladder, then do so. If you have to drive the graduation car you got as a gift until you start a family, then do so. Oftentimes, we get ourselves into unnecessary debt just to keep up with the world. It's less stressful for a couple when they do not have to borrow so much from others to live comfortably. Talk with your mate and decide what is important for you to have at the stage of life you are in together.

The Handling of Money

A couple may argue that one spends more than the other and it is the reason why they can never stay in their budget. The husband may think the wife is out shopping and maxing out credit cards, and the wife may think the husband is spending it on useless stuff for his ego. But, the truth is you can be spending over your budget and may think it is for good cause or reason, but you are actually spending about the same.

For most women, they tend to spend more money on things for the house, bills, food, clothes, etc. To a husband, that seems pretty reasonable, but if she were to spend it on a new wardrobe of clothes, accessories, more handbags, and a ton of shoes to fill her closet, then it would not seem reasonable. Most men tend to spend more for their hobbies, their interests, or simply just for their collections. It seems unreasonable to a woman, but let's say he spends money on a nice tennis bracelet as a gift to give to his loving wife. To a wife, that is not unreasonable. It is all coming out of the same budget and comes out to be about the same in price. So, no one is really spending more than the other, their viewpoint is just different on what the money is being spent for. What does God's perspective look like?

"Whoever loves money never has enough; whoever loves wealth is never satisfied with their income. This too is meaningless."

(Ecclesiastes 5:10, NIV)

In today's world, it always seems like there is simply not enough money to satisfy our so called "Needs" when they are actually just our desires. Prices on everything seem outrageous, so couples fight over who is spending more and not budgeting efficiently. It is dangerous for one spouse to love money more than the other, but it is even more dangerous if both spouses love money. They will not only feel like they do not have enough for themselves, but they will resent the other spouse for spending anything at all. As a couple, this is why merging is so important. If there is knowledge for both husband and wife of incoming money, then a budget can be in place and the handling of money can be on the same accord. Of course, we want our needs met, but it is nice when we have been blessed with a little more to get our desires. Couples should not put blame on each other for the amount that is being spent. Instead, really sit down and talk about what needs to be taken care of first, then you can save up for the desirable big items for pleasure. Saving up for the desirable outcomes will be meaningful, because you had enough to take care of all the needs and then enough for *feel good* spending. It should be agreed upon on what is spent.

How Love Conquers Finances

Many of us have heard the expression "Money is the root of all evil." Well, that is not true. The Bible does not say that money is the root of all evil; it says the *love* of money is the root of all evil.

"For the love of money is the root of all evil: which while some coveted after, they have erred from the faith, and pierced themselves through with many sorrows."

(I Timothy 6:10, NIV)

When you read this passage, it makes perfect sense why money is the number one cause of problems in a marriage. The love of money keeps us from merging; the love of money keeps us in secrecy; the love of money gets us into debt; the love of money causes us to mishandle it; and the love of money causes many other problems in our marriage. Loving money is what causes us to err or go astray from faith. God wants us to put all of our faith in Him in all things, including money. Believing that money is what will keep us safe, protected, and prosperous is what the world wants us to believe, but God is the source of it all. It is God who will provide everything you need and more, but He expects you to do one of the most important things with money and that is to tithe from your earnings in all thanksgiving. He loves a cheerful giver.

"Remember this: Whoever sows sparingly will also reap sparingly, and whoever sows generously will also reap generously. Each of you should give what you have decided in your heart to give, not reluctantly or under compulsion, for God loves a cheerful giver."

(2 Corinthians 9:6-7, NIV)

In the Old Testament, there is a guideline of how much to tithe and that is ten percent of your earnings. You can read the passage on your own, *Numbers 18:21-28.* However, in the New Testament it does not mention a specific amount to give. It simply explains that according to how much you give, you will reap. When you give to the Kingdom of God, decide through the Holy Spirit what the right amount is to give. Be excited and thankful that you are able to give, and give out of a generous heart. A millionaire would more than likely have plenty of room to give generously, but if they chose to give a dollar or two of their earnings, do you think they would find great gratitude in giving that much? It's definitely not something to shout about. But, let's take someone who has very little money and barely has enough to get by to pay the bills. To be able to give a dollar or a few more is giving generously. It is to show gratitude and faith in God. Ten percent is a guideline, but God looks at your heart when it comes to giving. Because we are saved by grace and not by works, it is because of this that we should want to give generously. So, a great conquer against finances is to give God all the glory in your financial situations by giving to His Kingdom first, and in return, you will receive the wisdom you need to be able to sustain your finances in your marriage with great blessing and prosperity that is controlled. You will reap what you sow and the more you give, the more you will receive. Instead of loving money, love what God has done for you and give back generously. Make God a priority throughout your marriage in finances and then gain wisdom of what is expected of you in the areas of finances, so your marriage will be at peace in that area.

While you are engaged, observe how your mate handles money but most importantly, talk about it. It is very vital to know these things before you get married.

Reflection Questions:

Question 1: How much debt is each of you bringing into this relationship? Have you discussed it?

Question 2: Do you have an action plan on how you are going to get married with limited debt? What is the plan?

Question 3: What is your view on tithing? Do you come into agreement about it?

Question 4: What are your views on merging money?

Chapter 9

Against Lack of Communication

At any point of your life, have you ever asked the question on whether or not you are hearing from God? I have asked this question over and over again and sometimes desperately hoped that He would just come right out and audibly speak to me in the way we do, as humans. Communicating to one another clearly, loudly, and consistently through a back and forth conversation. I mean, He has audibly spoken to Adam in the Garden (Genesis 3:9), through a burning bush to Moses, a bright light with Saul, etc. So, when I am desperate to hear Him, I would reference those circumstances and say, "Why can't I hear clear from Him like they do all the time?"

Then one day, I was reminded of many years ago, the one and only time that I did hear an audible voice from Him and not only heard Him, but I heard Him and may have misinterpreted what He was trying to tell me. So, even though I heard from Him audibly, I was not really listening to what He was trying to say. What I thought He meant at that time, years later, I realized I must have misunderstood what He was trying to say. Because of this misinterpretation, I went throughout years believing it to mean one way and lived it out, when I could have taken it another way and saved years of hurt and pain. Why did I think I misunderstood? I misunderstood because I was a baby Christian at that time and I did not use every resource I had to understand what God was trying to tell me. I took His audible voice the way I wanted it to mean without seeking the true meaning behind it. One of the characteristics I had to learn the hard way about God is that He is straightforward when He speaks. But, because we are so complicated, we look into what He is trying to say more than we need to.

Communication is just as important to God to have with us as it is with each other, but we sometimes miss what He is trying to say, because we are not really listening. Our prayers can become one-sided, because we are doing all the talking. There are several ways He communicates with us; through His written Word, the Bible; through nature, through people, through dreams or visions, songs, through genuine prayer, and most importantly, through the Holy Spirit. These are some of the ways God communicates with us, but for many of us, we do not take the time to really listen and take in what He is trying to tell us. We lack the real intimate communication that God wants us to have with Him. If we could master communication with God, then my goodness, He could really take us on an amazing journey, according to His will and purpose for us. Communication with Him is vital for our entire life.

As couples, communication is such a vital factor that is needed in the relationship, too, but is often the hardest. There are many reasons that make communication difficult. The links of communicating could become forms of manipulating, criticizing, condemning, and mechanisms of defending. Communicating can also lead to over-exerting conversations, pacifying conversations to shut it down, uncompromising circles of unending results, and misunderstandings. Like I said earlier, God is straightforward, but we are complicated. I say this, because since we are complicated, we complicate communication. It makes sense why He does not audibly just talk to us the way I always hoped He would, like we do as humans to each other. If He did, we could find ourselves wrestling with God in the same manner with communicating like we do as humans. But, with Him being straightforward and us seeking to find His answers in the way we do, it leaves no room for a complicated long drawn out process of communicating with Him. He says it and we can choose to listen and accept, or disregard and reject. The choice is ours, but His answer stays the same, end of discussion.

So, how can couples come to a point where it's not so complicated? The answer is pretty simple.

"My dear brothers and sisters, take note of this: Everyone should be quick to listen, slow to speak and slow to become angry."

(James 1:19, NIV)

Quick to Listen

I remember one day when we were younger, my brother and I were talking about some random stuff and at some point, and he interrupted me, to say, "Have you ever noticed that we always do that in our family?" I said, "Notice what?" He was referring to us interrupting each other while talking. It was funny when he pointed it out, because I never really noticed it; it was just something we did in our family. It did not matter if it was my mom talking, my dad talking, or one of us talking. We just never let each other finish a complete sentence, because we were too excited to jump in on the conversation and say what came to mind. Well, ever since then, I noticed it and thought to myself how we actually never really modeled the, "quick to listen and slow to speak," message. Of course, it was never an issue while we were just having fun in conversation, but when there was any kind of conflict in the house, then interrupting was noticed and corrected. As time went on, we did start to take notice of our interrupting habit and had to learn how to be *quick to listen and slow to speak*, whether it was fun in conversation or serious talks.

For some of us, learning how to be quick to listen is hard, because out of impulse, we want to say what we need to say to make our point. But, if you want to have good communication with your mate, then listening is going to be the most important aspect to learning everything you need to know about them, in order to keep moving forward in your relationship with full understanding.

Listening to your mate is one of the highest needs when communicating successfully. It's the highest because it is often the need we choose to ignore. We choose to ignore listening to our mate, because of the pride in our hearts. Like I said earlier, you are two different people with different philosophies trying to come together. You each are going to have disagreements, feelings about how to be treated, views on how things should be handled, and views on what is right and wrong. In some relationships, we have differences on the complete opposite ends of the stick. We keep trying to express our differences, but because we are so far apart on the stick, we can't hear each other and we are not willing to scoot closer inward of the stick, so we can get a clear understanding of what the other is trying to say. Instead, we would rather stay on the opposite end and keep expressing our own differences, thinking we are getting heard.

"Fools find no pleasure in understanding but delight in airing their own opinions."

(Proverbs 18:2, NIV)

When our mate is trying to address an issue in our relationship, oftentimes, instead of trying to listen to what the issue is and how it can be resolved, we try and project our own opinions or our own issues against the initial issues. Nothing gets resolved this way. It's almost like little children trying to fight for their spot of attention. I have two kids who love to tell their stories. It is definitely easier when I have one at a time, because I can focus on just one story. But, there are those rare times when they are both in the same room with me and both have stories to tell. One will start a story and the other will have a story that they experienced similarly, and interrupt. They are both eager to tell their stories, because it is very important to them. I love hearing their stories, but when they are trying to compete for their spot to tell them, it kills the flow of storytelling, because I have to correct them and say, "Wait until it is your turn, so that I can hear both of your stories." When they are able to wait on their turn, then I can react to their story in the way that lets them know I was actively listening to it.

A more serious example is when America protests against issues. Recently, in the year 2016, people all over the world were protesting that *Black Lives Matter*. Too many people were agreeing that there was injustice of racial profiling and police brutality that caused several African American deaths and were getting away with it. Many people of all races were coming together, so they could be heard on that one issue. People were walking in streets, crowding outside police stations, and some famous athletes stood on their knees, while the *Star Spangled Banner* played. They believed that for that time period, the *Black Lives Matter* needed to be the primary focus. Granted, police brutality has been known and can happen to any race; however, the focus was on black lives, because videos were being circulated to show how cops were killing black people, and all of them got off. But, while black lives were the primary focus, others decided that, no, it should not be *Black Lives Matter*, but it should be *All Lives Matter*. No videos circulated to show racial profiling and police brutality killings towards any other race. So, why it became *Black Lives Matter* to *All Lives Matter* did not make sense to many protestors. The *Black Lives Matter* groups felt like they were not getting heard and that America was not listening, when others decided all lives matter. In addition to this, others were voicing their own opinions about how black people need to comply or that black people are always angry anyway. It caused racial tensions and retaliation. After *Black Lives Matter*, then *All Lives Matter* came *Blue Lives Matter*, because cops were getting killed unjustly, as well.

The point of this is that initially, the issue was *Black Lives Matter* and the diverse protest group felt like it was time to be heard, but because others disagreed with it for one reason or another, they tried to take the focus away from the initial issue. Later, it was found that Americans who protested *Black Lives Matter* were not fighting in vain and they were being heard, because America's second largest police department, located in Chicago, did, in fact, reveal a 183 page report that validated "the widely held belief that police have no regard for the sanctity of life when it comes to people of color." There were more shocking findings, which you can read on the website provided, but the findings is not the focus. This example just goes to show you how when an issue arises that someone feels the need to be addressed and heard, how easily the focus can be taken away, because of opinions, retaliation, and lack of understanding or listening.

Slow to Speak

It's apparent that in our relationships, there will be times when there is an issue that needs to be addressed. What needs to be evaluated is the issue, who is causing the issue, and how the issue can be resolved. One other thing to remember is that if one of you is addressing an issue, listen to that issue and try not to project your issue at the same time. Be slow to speak. In other words, take turns on addressing the issues. If an issue has been brought to you, take time to focus on just that issue, because that is what needs to be focused on for the moment. Your time will come, but if your issue is not related to the issue on the table, then don't add to it. Don't add hurtful opinions, don't disregard the issue, don't bring up the past, and don't think the issue is ridiculous, just listen and hear what transformation needs to take place in order to bring the issue to peace. Yes, it is hard for most of us, especially if the issue is something we caused. The first thing many of us try to do is taking the focus off of our doing and make the focus about something else, often turning it the other way around. It's a hurtful cycle and until we can learn how to really listen to the issue, big or small, nothing will change and nothing will be understood. But, when we humble ourselves to really listen; we can think more clearly on how to resolve it with acceptance, dignity, and grace, in order to be able to speak about it in a respectful manner.

When learning how to be slow to speak, absorb what you are hearing and then process it before speaking. If you have to ask questions to help you understand what you are hearing, then do so. But, do not speak to be defensive right away. If you are offended by what you are hearing, evaluate why you are offended, and then of course, let them know that you are, but in a respectful manner.

Slow to Anger

We already discussed how God loves, but just to touch up on it, it took so much before Jesus got angry and when He did, it was against evil doings. We are entitled to get angry when necessary, but make sure your anger is strictly against something that truly is evil. Some of us get angry over the littlest of things and do not always control it. As a parent, I am sure that many of you can relate. I have two kids and no matter how many times you teach and tell them how to clean their room, it does not always get done as you expect it to be done. So often, when I go in their room and see a slight mess or a huge mess, I get so angry, because I just can't understand why it is so hard to do such simple tasks. As parents, we all want to teach our kids responsibility and make sure that they will take these habits into adulthood. But, as I got older with them, I started to understand one thing and that was how to give grace with this issue. I have always grown up to believe that I took care of my room. For the most part, I did, but as I got older into my adult years, I did not always keep my room in perfect condition. When I evaluated why, I look as far back as college when I got busy with school and working throughout college, cleaning my room did not become my ultimate priority, because I was too tired to clean at my best. It got cleaned, but not to my best.

When I got married and had kids, it got worse trying to keep it to my cleanest. However, when I had kids, I was determined that they understood to make sure they kept their room to my standards. When it did not happen all the time, I would get so angry and have these outbursts of anger towards them. Not exactly proud of my consistent shouting above my lung capacity, or the many overly exaggerated punishment withholdings, but I did get overly angry. So, I had to step back and evaluate my anger in it. Did I have a right to be angry about it, yes, but I also had to understand what was going on with them. Here is what I understood; we always made sure that they were involved with something to keep them busy, such as sports, or activities. Well, as they got older, those very things that we made a part of their lives became more demanding, in addition to their schoolwork, and eventually, having a paying job for themselves. How can I expect them to keep their room in perfect condition on a daily basis, when I myself have a hard time keeping mine in perfect condition, because of all my duties throughout the day? It became a double standard and I had to give them grace or I would find myself being angry at them all the time, instead of showing them love all the time. So, I had to learn how to be angry in a loving manner to address what is not right, but give them grace at the same time.

When I finally realized the importance of being a grace-filled parent, that is when my stress levels went down and it alleviated the anger outbursts. What really allowed me to become a grace-filled parent was to know that our Father in Heaven is a grace-filled Papa. We, too, will always do things that are not pleasing to Him, but He deals with it in a loving manner and does it with grace until eventually, we get it. The one thing that He will get angry about is anything that is truly evil. He does not get angry when we make mistakes, when we don't listen, when we are stubborn, or when we flat out do stupid things. He may get disappointed, but not so angry that He will deny us. We have consequences for our actions, but the only time He will get so angry is if we completely deny His goodness and consciously turn to evil. As a parent, I just had to learn how to address the concerns without the anger outbursts and know when to get angry with grace.

I used my children as an example to be slow to anger, but this does apply to our relationships with our mates, too. Our mates will make mistakes, will do things we just don't understand, and will do things that do not fall in line with our standards, but learn how to be angry about it with grace. If you are getting angry in an unproductive manner such as abuse, then some major evaluation needs to be examined by the both of you. There may be some deep rooted issues that have not been out in the open and it may be something you will need to take into consideration before you say, "I do".

The simplest way not to get to unproductive anger is to be *quick to listen and slow to speak*. By doing these two things, you will find less of the unreasonable anger outbursts.

Reflection Questions:

Question 1: How well do you feel like you and your mate communicate?

Question 2: Is there room for improvement and if so, what will it take for the both of you to improve that?

Chapter 10

Against the World, Before Saying, "I Do": Knowing True Love

"Beloved, let us [unselfishly] love and seek the best for one another, for love is from God; and everyone who loves [others] is born of God and knows God [through personal experience]. The one who does not love has not become acquainted with God [does not and never did know Him], for God is love. [He is the originator of love, and it is an enduring attribute of His nature.] By this the love of God was displayed in us, in that God has sent His [One and] only begotten Son [the One who is truly unique, the only One of His kind] into the world so that we might live through Him. In this is love, not that we loved God, but that He loved us and sent His Son to be the propitiation [that is, the atoning sacrifice, and the satisfying offering] for our sins [fulfilling God's requirement for justice against sin and placating His wrath].

Beloved, if God so loved us [in this incredible way], we also ought to love one another. No one has seen God at any time. But if we love one another [with unselfish concern], God abides in us, and His love [the love that is His essence abides in us and] is completed and perfected in us. By this we know [with confident assurance] that we abide in Him and He in us, because He has given to us His [Holy] Spirit. We [who were with Him in person] have seen and testify [as eyewitnesses] that the Father has sent the Son to be the Savior of the world.

Whoever confesses and acknowledges that Jesus is the Son of God, God abides in him, and he in God. We have come to know [by personal observation and experience], and have believed [with deep, consistent faith] the love which God has for us. God is love, and the one who abides in love abides in God, and God abides continually in him. In this [union and fellowship with Him], love is completed and perfected with us, so that we may have confidence in the day of judgment [with assurance and boldness to face Him]; because as He is, so are we in this world. There is no fear in love [dread does not exist]. But perfect (complete, full-grown) love drives out fear, because fear involves [the expectation of divine] punishment, so the one who is afraid [of God's judgment] is not perfected in love [has not grown into a sufficient understanding of God's love]. We love, because He first loved us. If anyone says, "I love God," and hates (works against) his [Christian] brother he is a liar; for the one who does not love his brother whom he has seen, cannot love God whom he has not seen. And this commandment we have from Him, that the one who loves God should also [unselfishly] love his brother and seek the best for him.

(1 John 4:7-21, AMP)

I've been told many times that love is a choice. I do believe that it is a choice and that we should choose to love people, because God loves us. However, I do not believe that love is simply a basis on choosing to love. It is definitely a natural enduring feeling and it is also an action. I wanted to show you this scripture from the Amplified version of the Bible, because it is a complete description of God's love and our love. I wanted to really break this scripture down, because once you understand what this scripture truly means, then you will see if you have true love for one another. 1 Corinthians definition of love shows you the kind of love you should have for one another, but this scripture in the book of John will show you if you have *true love* and the love that will sustain your relationship as a couple.

"Beloved, let us [unselfishly] love and seek the best for one another, for love is from God; and everyone who loves [others] is born of God and knows God [through personal experience]. The one who does not love has not become acquainted with God [does not and never did know Him], for God is love. [He is the originator of love, and it is an enduring attribute of His nature.]"

(1 John 4:7-8, NIV)

First things first, love is an unselfish act. When you love, it is not to gain anything for yourself. But, instead, love always seeks the best for one another. When you love someone, you genuinely want to see that every area of their life reaches the fullest potential of being at its best. This is how God loves, because He is the ultimate definition of love. This kind of love comes from God and God alone. So, if you have this kind of love from God and are able to share and express this kind of love to others, then it is because you know God.

Hopefully, you have full understanding of the definition of what love looks like, so what does it look like when you don't love? In this first part of the scripture, it stresses to love unselfishly. When someone loves selfishly, then they are dedicated to caring for themselves and only seek their own interest, or welfare, above anyone else. The motive behind anything that is done is to benefit oneself. It is hard to love someone who does not know how to love unselfishly. But, many relationships are unbalanced in this. One is a selfish lover and the other is an unselfish lover. Oftentimes, the unselfish lover will feel like they are being taken for granted.

Observe what your motives are when you love someone or better yet, what are the motives behind your mate when it comes to loving you? People all over have misunderstood what love is and can easily love someone for their own selfish desires or fall in love with someone who impersonated a false sense of love. It could be for the love of money, the lustful desires of sex, comfort in companionship, or the fear of being alone, etc. In some motives to love, it is to make someone feel good about themselves to cover up any kind of shame they have hidden in their heart. All of these reasons are selfish.

Loving selfishly will eventually die out. Years will pass and an unfulfilling relationship will fester like cancer until one day, you realize that the love you thought you had is not enough. There is only one kind of love that lasts forever and that is God's love. When His love is in you and you in Him, then the love is enduring and unselfish.

God is the first to ever love. Since God is love, His love is a natural attribution that lasts forever and never changes. It is because of His natural ability to love that He did not choose to love us; but, He created us out of love. He carefully and wonderfully created us out of His love and in His image, which means that we have the ability to love and be loved like Him. If a person does not love, then they do not have a personal relationship with God.

"By this the love of God was displayed in us, in that God has sent His [One and] only begotten Son [the One who is truly unique, the only One of His kind] into the world so that we might live through Him. In this is love, not that we loved God, but that He loved us and sent His Son to be the propitiation [that is, the atoning sacrifice, and the satisfying offering] for our sins [fulfilling God's requirement for justice against sin and placating His wrath]. Beloved, if God so loved us [in this incredible way], we also ought to love one another."

(1 John 4:9-11, NIV)

There is no greater love than what God has done. Not only as our Heavenly Father did He send His Son to take the fall for our sinful nature, but He, in the flesh, took the beating. It is because of His love for us, why He sent His Son. When He created us out of love in His image, He still gave us free will and, unfortunately, we have all used that free will to sin against His plans for us. Our selfishness causes us to go astray and fall short of understanding God's love for us. By God sending Jesus to the fallen world of our sinfulness, this was God's way of ensuring the best for us. He did not want us to stay in our sinful nature. But instead, He wanted us to stay in His grace and love. Once we truly understand the sacrifices and the purposes of God, who is for us, we then desire to love Him. Not only do we have this strong desire to love God, but we have a strong desire to love others, as well.

"No one has seen God at any time. But if we love one another [with unselfish concern], God abides in us, and His love [the love that is His essence abides in us and] is completed and perfected in us. By this we know [with confident assurance] that we abide in Him and He in us, because He has given to us His [Holy] Spirit. We [who were with Him in person] have seen and testify [as eye-witnesses] that the Father has sent the Son to be the Savior of the world. Whoever

confesses and acknowledges that Jesus is the Son of God, God abides in him, and he in God. We have come to know [by personal observation and experience], and have believed [with deep, consistent faith] the love which God has for us. God is love, and the one who abides in love abides in God, and God abides continually in him. In this [union and fellowship with Him], love is completed and perfected with us, so that we may have confidence in the day of judgment [with assurance and boldness to face Him]; because as He is, so are we in this world."

(1 John 4:12-14, NIV)

This scripture makes it very clear over and over that when we accept Jesus into our life, we can begin to understand His love for us. After we truly experience the redemption from our Savior, we receive the Holy Spirit within us. It is amazing how we are able to experience this love for each other and have never even seen what He looks like. So, why are we able to experience a deep love for God when we have never seen Him? The Holy Spirit that dwells in us is God's love within us and because of that; we are able to receive His love and also love back. This sums up why His love abides in us and we abide in His love perfectly and in completeness. When His love truly abides in us, we cannot help but to love Him and also other people with a sincere heart and with unselfish intentions.

"There is no fear in love [dread does not exist]. But perfect (complete, full-grown) love drives out fear, because fear involves [the expectation of divine] punishment, so the one who is afraid [of God's judgment] is not perfected in love [has not grown into a sufficient understanding of God's love]. We love, because He first loved us."

(1 John 4:18-19, NIV)

I wanted to pay close attention to the part of this scripture that says we love, because He first loved us. As mentioned earlier, people say love is a choice. I say initially, yes, it is a choice, but, the choice is driven by a feeling, then an action. Everything that God did is driven by His love for us.

Many of us have acknowledged at one point of our early lives that there is a God. I am not talking about those of us who grew up in a Christian home where they made God the focal point of their lives. I am talking about those of us who did not grow up in church or study the Bible in our home, as children. We knew as children that there was a God, but, many of us did not have a true experience with Him until our later years. But, when you finally come to an experience of knowing who God is and the Agape love that He has for you, you can't help but to want to love Him back.

I remember when I was fourteen-years-old, I had a dream that I was staring out of my window and I saw an image of Jesus in the clouds holding His arms open wide, as if He was inviting me to come hug Him. Prior to that dream, I knew Him because of family members who would occasionally talk about Him or had pictures, but I did not know you could have a personal relationship with Him, and I did not understand the magnitude of who God was to me personally. I just knew that in my dream, it was Him. The next day, I was brought to a mall and while I was walking through the mall, I saw the same image on a painting that was in my dream; Jesus in the clouds inviting me. Within that week, I saw several more pictures and paintings with that same image. I did not know exactly what that meant back then, but I had a strong desire to want to know about Jesus. That feeling lasted for some time, but it was not until I was seventeen when I was asked by a pastor that I met, "Are you saved?" I told him no, and I didn't think so. The pastor who explained it to me prayed over me and we prayed the Savior's prayer. I became a Christian at seventeen, but even then, I did not know that you had to read the Bible and go to church regularly, in order to be fed the Word of God and nurture the Holy Spirit within. So, I continued to live my life as a carnal Christian.

One year, I was going through so many emotions dealing with school, relationships, and family members. It was one thing after another, and I found myself to be alone dealing with it. I began watching TBN at that time and started to come to a little bit of an understanding of how much God loves. The Holy Spirit was starting to become ignited in me and I wanted to do things right, but I still did not quite understand the whole dynamic of having a genuine relationship with God. Anything I did was more so out of legalism and fear of doing things wrong towards God. It was not until after I got married in a relationship that God did not join together, when I realized just how much God loved me. The relationship started off awful for both of us and he winded up leaving me for another woman. Back then, I was seeking so much for God's will for my life, but because I was still a baby Christian, I still did not understand what that really meant. However, there was one thing that I did know during that time of my life and that was that God loved me. Simply because of that, I began to desire God more and loved Him more. My feelings for God changed and I began to want nothing but Him in my messed up life. It was a feeling I had for Him, because He showed me that despite the mess I was in from my own selfishness, He loved me. Not only did I love Him more, but I started to love other people, despite who they were towards me. Particularly, at that time, I chose to love my husband, because God loved Him, too. I did not choose to love him because I felt loved by him, but I chose to love him, because we were still married and I loved God. I chose to try and stay in the marriage loving my husband, even when he did not love me the way I should have been loved by him. When you have God's love in you, you choose to love other people, despite who they are. How it ends up is another story for another chapter in my life that will be revealed in another book. But, for now, I just wanted to show how when you love, it is because God loved you first. It is God's love that ignites the Spirit within to love.

I share this story to show that no matter what type of background people grow up in; God has a way of revealing who He is to you, simply because He loves you. When you experience His love, you then have an initial choice and that is to accept His love or reject it. Once you choose Him and His love for you, then you experience and feel the love from Him that abides in you and you in Him. You don't just wake up one day and say, "I think I am going to choose to love God today." You choose to love Him, because of who He is and you choose to love Him, because you are drawn to want to love Him for His goodness and His agape love towards you. So, when people say love is a choice, it is, but not in the sense of you waking up every day to force yourself to love. We love Him, we love others, because God loved us first.

Hopefully, when you choose a mate that you plan on spending a lifetime with, it is because you know in your heart that you are genuinely loved by this person and you are genuinely in love with this person. We love God because we know that we are genuinely loved by Him. Who would not want to love someone like that? It is the same when choosing a mate. That is not to say that there will not be times when you can't stand them for whatever reason, but when there is genuine, sincere, and unselfish love, then love is what pushes through those moments.

Scripture says that there is no fear in love. I love how the amplified extends to say that dread does not exist in love. When you really think about that statement, if God is love and all love, then we should never feel any kind of dreadfulness in Him. Whoever says I dread loving God? If you fear God in any way, then you do not believe His love for you. His love is made in complete perfection when we are truly in Him, and there is no reason why we should dread loving Him or be fearful of Him. Likewise, in your relationship, there should be no dreadful feelings in loving someone or receiving love from them. If you have dreadful feelings in any way, whether it is dreading to trust them, dreading to be intimate with them, dreading their intentions, or dreading to be with them, then some evaluations need to be taken into consideration. What would cause any hesitation to love one another?

"If anyone says, "I love God," and hates (works against) his [Christian] brother he is a liar; for the one who does not love his brother whom he has seen, cannot love God whom he has not seen. And this commandment we have from Him, that the one who loves God should also [unselfishly] love his brother and seek the best for him."

(1 John 4:20, NIV)

This sums up what this chapter is about. You cannot say you love God, but not show it for others. It is impossible to show genuine love for one another if you do not truly love God. This is what it means to be a Christian. A Christian is *Christ-like*. When you think about how Christ loves, it is such a powerful love. He loves with full intent to give His best interests for us. His love is the driving force for our well-being. His love is our total existence. So, with complete confidence, you know it is true love when you are both complete in Christ. This is why it is so important that you truly know what it looks like when someone calls themselves a Christian. Anyone can say they are a Christian, but their actions in love will definitely show just how much of a *Christian* they truly are. If God is love, then anything outside of God is not love. Yes, there is the world's standard of love, but the one and greatest true love is the love from and through God, in order to love one another.

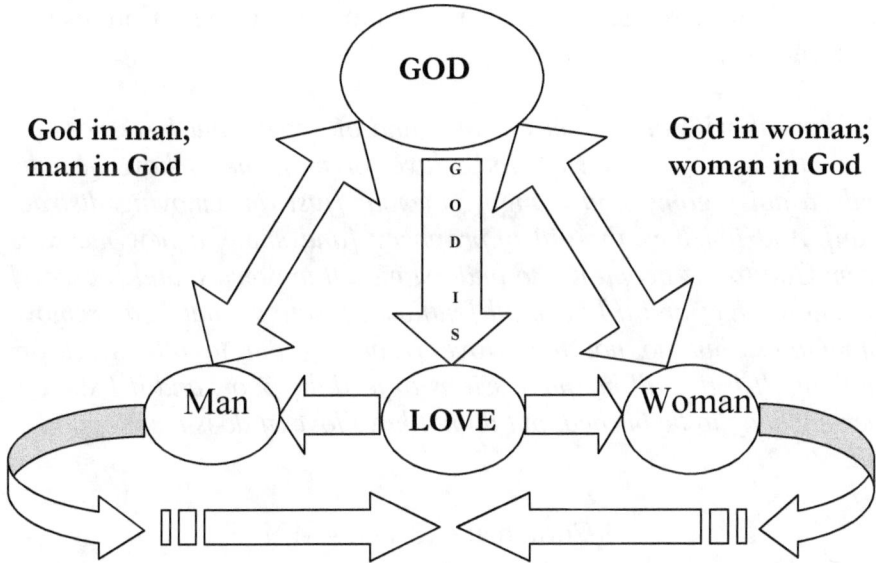

God is love; when man and woman are both in God and God in them, then God's love pours out and you are loving each other through God's enduring, everlasting, and perfect love as a couple.

It is plain to see that when both of you have God's love, then you will be able to sustain so much more than you can imagine as a couple. But, if only one of you have God's love in you, or if both of you do not have God's love, then it will be more of a challenge to stay in love with each other in such a way that reaches the ultimate fulfillment in love.

I have heard many pastors say that marriage is for Christians. It took a while for me to really understand what that meant. It does not mean that everyone is excluded from marrying if you are not a Christian. What that means is that when one man and one woman fully understand who they are as individuals in Christ and understand God's love, then they are able to have the Holy Matrimony that God intended for marriages to become with sincere love. The love that pours out into them from Christ will allow them to love one another with the deepest strength, in order to overcome the obstacles that will arise in their marriage. Which brings me to two closing scriptures that seal true love.

"If I speak with the tongues of men and of angels, but have not love [for others growing out of God's love for me], then I have become only a noisy gong or a clanging cymbal [just an annoying distraction]. And if I have the gift of prophecy [and speak a new message from God to the people], and understand all mysteries, and [possess] all knowledge; and if I have all [sufficient] faith so that I can remove mountains, but do not have love [reaching out to others], I am nothing. If I give all my possessions to feed the poor, and if I surrender my body to be burned, but do not have love, it does me no good at all."

(1 Corinthians 13:1-3, AMP)

We can fall in love with a person who has charisma and speaks with beautiful eloquence like angels sent from heaven, but if they don't have love, then it is merely a person pacifying or appeasing you. We can fall in love with someone who knows the Bible from front to back and can tell you everything they have read or a person who has five degrees and has a mind like a scientist, but if they don't have love, then it means nothing. They could have faith that believes that all will be well and nothing is impossible, but if they do not have love, then their faith means nothing. A person could be giving and have no problem doing so, doing good for others, volunteering their time for others, giving to every charity imaginable, but if they do not have love, then their giving is in vain. A person can sacrifice their physical being for someone else and lay down their life to rescue a person, as if they were a firefighter or cop, but if they have no love, then giving up of oneself means absolutely nothing. A person can be an amazing, wonderful, and giving person, but if they do not have love, then their worth means nothing. These are powerful statements, because we can say completely that God is love and love is God, and a person who is all these good things, but does not have God, then he/she does not truly know love. As stated earlier, anything without God is not love.

"And now there remain: faith [abiding trust in God and His promises], hope [confident expectation of eternal salvation], love [unselfish love for others growing out of God's love for me], these three [the choicest graces]; but the greatest of these is love."

(1 Corinthians 13:13, AMP)

The greatest is *love*. Why? Because, God is love and He is the greatest. But, if you are not in God and He is not in you, then you do not have the greatest love that allows you to grow together as a couple gracefully. God's love is true and pure. Isn't that the kind of love you want in each other?

For many of us, we are so quick to simply *fall in love* with someone. We may get a love that is acceptable, but many of us miss out on a love that is an amazing kind of love. A love that does not grow weary, a love that is persistent, a love that conquers, a love that says we can get through this, and a love that says, "I do, forever." When you have love based on God's definition of love in 1 Corinthians 13:4-7 and a love that is from God in 1 John 4:7-21 then you can have true love and a love that will say, "We are one, until death do us part." Anything else is not God's best.

Reflection Questions:

Question 1: Can you honestly say that you and your mate, as individuals, make God your priority? How do you know?

Question 2: How do you view God in your life?

Question 3: List the ways that you love unselfishly? List the ways you love selfishly?

Question 4: Are there any fears that you have about marrying your mate? Why or why not?

Question 5: Do you feel like your mate has your best interests at all times and in all areas of your life? Why or why not?

Question 6: What does reaching oneness look like to you? Is it attainable in your relationship?

Conclusion

Getting married is very exciting and it should be one of the many greatest joys in life. However, it is also one of the greatest decisions that need to be taken very seriously. Marriage is God's will for your life. He wants you to have a marriage that is fulfilling and for it to reach the oneness that He desires for you to have, but marrying someone who is not God's will for your life can be one of the biggest mistakes you make. There are guidelines to what God lays out when choosing a mate and it is His best for you, so why not desire His best? It is not to say that His best for you will not go through trials and tribulations, but even so, you want to be with His best, so that you both can get through them with pure intentions and sincere focus to the end. Too many of us miss out on His best only to live with regrets and misery. For those of us who have or are experiencing this type of grief, yes, there is still hope that He will make the path straight. But, for those of you who are thinking about getting married, then by all means, please know what you are getting into, so that you do not fall into the same category of grief. You want to make sure that you have *true love* before committing to forever. May you seek God wholeheartedly in your decision to marry and may God reveal His best for you. Blessings!

ABOUt tHE AUtHOR

Catherine Harmon is a mother and an author, with a Bachelors degree in Psychology. Her first book was published in 2009, entitled, *I do...Until Death do us Part?* However, it is currently off the market due to revisions. In 2017, she published another book that is established as the first book of a series entitled, *Us Against the World*. This book series will contain the difficulties we face when going *against the world* during different seasons of our lives. The first book in the series was specifically for married couples, particularly those trying to overcome difficult obstacles, but in this second book of the series, it focuses on couples who are engaged. It was because of her marriage experience that has created a passion for people to understand God's desire for marriage, and that is to start off with His desire, so you can choose wisely when selecting a mate.

Catherine was married for nineteen years before she decided in 2017 to separate from her marriage for biblical reasons. Through her nineteen years of marriage, she gained the much needed wisdom to help couples understand the importance of a Christ-centered marriage. She is a huge advocate for marriage, but wants people to understand that both people in the marriage have to be on one accord with Christ, in order to have a healthier and successful marriage. The failures that took place in her marriage are more the reason why she wants couples to succeed, but to succeed with full understanding of God's love.

As she goes through her current journey, she continues to write the books in this series as a healing process to completeness in God's goodness. Her next book in the series focuses on the divorced and separated. Please look for the next books in this series, *Us Against the World*, as follows:

Books already published:

❖ Us Against the World... How God's Love Conquers All: For Married Couples

- ❖ Us Against the World…Before Saying, "I Do," Knowing True Love: For Engaged Couples

Books in the making:

- ❖ Us Against the World… God Hates Divorce, but Loves you More: For the Divorced and Separated
- ❖ Us Against the World… Naturally Rebellious, but Loved: For Teens
- ❖ Us Against the World… Embracing God's Love: For Singles

If you need prayer or have questions, Catherine is available and can be reached at againsttheworld.love@gmail.com.

BIBLIOGRaPHY

Books:

Hunter, Deborah G. *Holy Spirit: The Promise Left for the Believer.* Hunter Entertainment Network. Colorado Springs, Colorado, 2016

The Holy Bible, New International Version Life Application Study Bible. Grand Rapids. Zondervan. 2012. Print.

The Holy Bible, King James Version. New York. American Bible Society. 1999

The Holy Bible, Amplified Version. La Habra, CA 90631. The Lockman Foundation. 2015

Websites:

Sanchez, Ray. "No Regard': 7 Stark Findings on Chicago Police Treatment of Blacks and Latinos." CNN. April 15, 2016.

http://www.cnn.com/2016/04/15/us/chicago-police-task-force-disturbing-findings/index.html.

Television shows:

"Beyond Repair: Marriage in Crises." Iyanla, *Fix My Life.* OWN. USA. December 2017.